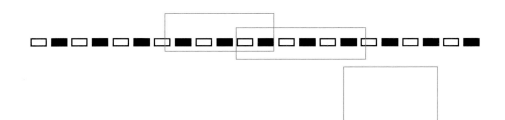

# The Art of
# the Storyboard

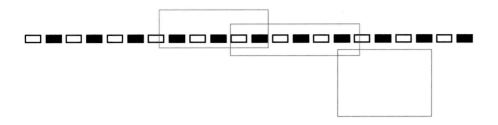

# The Art of
# the Storyboard

## A Filmmaker's Introduction

John Hart

ELSEVIER

AMSTERDAM • BOSTON • HEIDELBERG • LONDON
NEW YORK • OXFORD • PARIS • SAN DIEGO
SAN FRANCISCO • SINGAPORE • SYDNEY • TOKYO
Focal Press is an imprint of Elsevier

**Focal Press**

| Acquisitions Editor: | Georgia Kennedy |
| Publishing Services Manager: | George Morrison |
| Senior Project Manager: | Brandy Lilly |
| Assistant Editor: | David Bowers |
| Marketing Manager: | Marcel Koppes |
| Cover Design: | Alan Studholme |

Focal Press is an imprint of Elsevier
30 Corporate Drive, Suite 400, Burlington, MA 01803, USA
Linacre House, Jordan Hill, Oxford OX2 8DP, UK

 Recognizing the importance of preserving what has been written, Elsevier prints its books on acid-free paper whenever possible.

**Library of Congress Cataloging-in-Publication Data**
Application submitted

**British Library Cataloguing-in-Publication Data**
A catalogue record for this book is available from the British Library.

ISBN: 978-0-240-80960-1

For information on all Focal Press publications
visit our website at www.books.elsevier.com

07 08 09 10 11 5 4 3 2 1

Printed in the United States of America

Working together to grow
libraries in developing countries

www.elsevier.com | www.bookaid.org | www.sabre.org

ELSEVIER    BOOK AID
            International    Sabre Foundation

# Contents

To my dear friend, Mary Ann Maurer, whose professionalism, humor and positive outlook made writing this book such a pleasant task.

# Acknowledgements

I would like to acknowledge my late friend Lanny Foster, who is represented in this book.

A particular mention goes to Georgia Kennedy from Focal Press and Beth Millett, development editor, for their help and encouragement.

A majority of the artwork was drawn by me, unless otherwise noted for guest artists.

# Introduction

"What goes around comes around" couldn't be more applicable than to the recent announcement from Ed Catmull, president of Pixar and Disney Animation Studios, and John Lasseter, the chief creative officer, that they are once again returning to hand-drawn animation for their film projects. Hooray!

After the success of their computer-animated project *Toy Story* in 1995, they closed their hand-drawing facility in 2004. They have now decided, rightly, that the charm, linear attributes and added depth of hand-drawn animation still have a strong role to play in the future of animation. We wish them well — and the same to all of us artists who draw by hand!

**While I was studying art in high school, I thought the greatest place to get a job as an artist would be the Walt Disney Studios. Enthralled by the stunning visuals of Disney's *Snow White and the Seven Dwarfs*, followed by *Fantasia, Dumbo, Bambi,* and then the delightful *Song of the South* (the first to combine live action actors with cartoons), I very much wanted to be a part of Walt's creative force. Instead I got a fellowship and went for my Master's Degree in Fine Arts. I eventually got to New York rather than California and became a successful commercial artist/photographer/lecturer and author. Still, I wonder what would have happened had I been accepted in Walt's workshops.**

**I later learned that most of the artists on Walt's creative team simply worked at coloring the hundreds of thousands of cels (acetate sheets) that comprise a full-length cartoon. Those cel painters, called "in betweeners," actually went on strike a couple of times for more money. Now, if one had the talent to get a job in animation as an idea person, a concept sketch artist, a production design artist, a storyboard artist, or a character design person, that would have been a different story and a more creative one. As a matter of fact, concept artists are still in demand at Dreamworks and Pixar, as well as all the major film producers. With film production being a collaborative art, it's nice to see storyboard artists now getting acknowledged in the credits rolls on most major motion picture releases.**

Your drawing talents must be developed thoroughly in both rendering live-action images realistically and in interpreting images as called for in animated films or videos. To be a storyboard artist is to illustrate the individual frames that make up the shots in a shooting script for animated feature films, industrial films or multimedia projects, and educational films. All these genres use storyboards in one form or another. You are part of the preproduction team and will work with producers, production designers, directors of photography and the special effects teams, but most of your storyboard work will be done with the director, whose vision of the project will guide the entire production team.

*The Art of the Storyboard II* seeks to help you in the following ways:

- To summarize the history and development of the storyboard and to clarify its adaptation and function as a viable visual tool for the creative team that produces live-action feature length films, animation films, cartoons, multimedia/industrial films, videos and documentaries.

- To provide basic exercises and illustrations to help you develop the drawing, drafting and design skills essential to creating an artist's style that will satisfy the needs of the director.

- To increase the appreciation of the storyboard as a preproduction tool for producers, directors, cinematographers, art directors, etc. in any media who are not familiar with its processes and purposes.

- To help the student of storyboarding or film techniques whose time or funds restrict participation in organized classes.

- To serve as a standard text or a supplementary text for established art or film studies at a secondary or college level or in film schools.

Stills from historically important films – from silent to sound – will be used throughout the text to illustrate their design qualities and "stopped action." These are actually parts of a storyboard, called "shots" or "stills" from key frames. Each of the chosen renderings, from almost 200 entertainment projects, will serve three basic functions:

- To place the film in its historical context in the evolution of film styles, particularly those nominated for or awarded Academy Awards for Best Picture, Best Cinematography, Best Production Design/Art Direction or Best Special Effects.

- To clarify each film's unique compositional qualities, such as its use of framing in the context of reproducing a three-dimensional reality on the screen.

- To delineate the dynamic placement of figures, use of camera angles (the point of view of a character often dictates the camera angle used), and the director of photography's or cinematographer's "painting with light" and the striking visuals created by light and shade (chiaroscuro).

The stills or shots that have been analyzed and interpreted serve as illustrated frames that make up the visual narrative that is the sequential action of the storyboard. These key frames – when filmed as individual shots then projected on a screen at

30 frames per second – induce a *persistence of vision* on the human retina, thus creating a "cinematic motion" in the viewer's perception.

The basic drawing techniques illustrated in this book will be applicable to any creative work the storyboard artist is assigned to do in the world of feature films, whether it involves the use of computer generated images, special effects and compositing or not.

The repeated emphasis of this book is that drawing the story concept is the storyboard artist's first responsibility and that even rudimentary drawing techniques can convey the narrative flow of a given film project. I hope that the extra emphasis given here will refine those techniques and add a professional polish to the artistic output of the future storyboard artist.

**PERSISTENCE OF VISION:**
Retention of an image on the human retina causing the illusion of motion in films.

# Chapter 1

## The Storyboard's Beginnings

The film industry's current use of *storyboards* as a preproduction, pre-visualization tool owes its humble beginnings to the original Sunday comics. Pioneers like Winsor McKay, whose *Gertie the Dinosaur* (see Figure 1-1) and animation of the *Sinking of the* Lusitania (1915) established him as the true originator of the animated cartoon as an art form. He paved the way for Disney and others.

The concept of telling a story through a series of sequential drawings actually goes back to Egyptian hieroglyphics, even back to the cave men's drawings of stampeding cattle. The Bayeux Tapestries (1050), woven on linen and depicting with brutal narrative action William the Conqueror's invasion of England, is still awe-inspiring and has its own claims to being some of our first "storyboards."

Charles Solomon's *History of Animation* begins much later with the traveling magic lantern shows of the 1600s and takes readers from the optical illusion of *Phantasmagoria* in the 1800s to the contemporary animated cartoon: from *Felix the Cat* and *Mickey Mouse* in the 1920s up to *Jurassic Park* and *The Lion King* in the 1990s. Lately, we've had the brilliant 3D effects of The *Incredibles* (2004), *Shrek (2001)* and *Madagascar* (2005).

Even with our concentration primarily on film in this new edition of *Art of the Story-board*, we still have to recall a late-19th century major contributor to cinema — George Méliès, the French conjurer, illusionist, theatrical set designer and magician whose films projected optical tricks and fantasies. His *Trip to the Moon* (1902), with its stunning imagery of a rocket going "splat!" in the eye of the moon, is still used for documentaries and commercials. His other films include *Cinderella* (1899) and *Joan of Arc* (1902), and generation after generation continues to be fascinated with Méliès' inventive film spectaculars. Other artists who paved the way for animation were Felix Messmer, whose mischievous *Felix the Cat* (1914) became the world's most popular cartoon character, and Max Fleischer, who is best known for his still popular Betty Boop character.

Let's not forget Ub Iwerks, credited by many as being the original concept artist for Mickey Mouse, who bore a striking resemblance to Ub's Oswald Rabbit. 1929 was the beginning of the so-called "Disney Era," which reigned through the early 40s, when the entire world fell in love with Mickey Mouse (now just a corporate icon), Donald Duck, Pluto and *Snow White and the Seven Dwarfs* (1938), the first full-length cartoon, brilliantly Technicolored and a giant money maker for Walt Disney.

STORYBOARD: The storyboard is the premiere preproduction, pre-visualization tool designed to give a frame-by-frame, shot-by-shot series of sequential drawings adapted from the shooting script. They are concept drawings that illuminate and augment the script narrative and enable the entire production team to organize all the complicated action required by the script before the actual filming is done to create the correct look for the finished film.

**Figure 1-1 Hart's sketch of Winsor McKay with Gertie the Dinosaur, the ancestor of the animated cartoon. McKay's hand-drawn style is still influencing Disney's animators.**

Unless you want to be chained to a computer, digitally rendering a *Madagascar III*, the bigger reward would be to connect with the world of film. You could be creating great storyboards while working with directors in the tradition of Griffith, Fellini, Hitchcock, Truffaut, Selznick, Welles, Hawks, Spielberg, Scorcese, etc.

The use of the storyboard is the premiere tool in preproduction on any project. Whether you work in animated or live-action film, the storyboard artist must still arrange the story in a logical narrative sequence. Eric Sherman states in *Directing the Film*, "The storyboard consists of making a series of sketches where every basic scene and every camera set up within the scene illustrated – it is a visual record of the film's appearance before shooting begins." In my book "Lighting for Action," written for the still photographer moving to video and film, I describe the storyboard as a tool designed to "give you a frame-by-frame, shot-by-shot, organized program for your shooting sequence (or, the shooting script)." Christian Metz, author of "Film Language," refers to the shot (the basic component of the storyboard) as the "basic unit of film meaning."

Artists who created those original Sunday funnies drew their cartoon in a logical narrative sequence; this, essentially, is still the task of the storyboard artist. The use of the storyboard is a premiere aid in planning a filmed live action or animated feature. In "The Film Experience: Elements of Motion Picture Art" (1968), Ron Huss and Norman Silverstein elaborate on the storyboard artist as one who, "guided by the Director, captures the actions and passions that will be translatable into film," that they involve "a continuity reminiscent of comic strips," and that they remain "primarily pictorial."

Working from the original story idea, storyboards enable the entire production team to organize all the complicated action depicted in the script, whether being rendered for live action films, animation, or commercials. They will illustrate what action each lifted shot contains. By doing one's own storyboards carefully and thoroughly, you know exactly what is going to be done before the actual filming begins – every shot and every camera angle, along with what lighting, sets and props will be used.

Memorable scenes and sets don't just happen. You need talented people to create them. And, on a live action project, every section of lumber and each pound of plaster used in the building of sets, every performer, every costume, and every crew member, has to be accounted for and paid. Germs of ideas and creative conferences involving the director, director of photography, set designer, and costume designer are part of this necessary preproduction process.

Dozens of other creative people are involved in the extremely complicated preproduction process. The producer acquires the story property in the first place and raises the money to produce it. Producing it requires actors, costumers, composers of the soundtrack, grips, and other technicians like the carpenters, painters, even traffic managers and drivers. The entire production enterprise can be quite mind-boggling long before it is shot, edited, promoted and distributed to local movie theaters. The whole operation is doubly impressive when one considers the logistics of getting together this group of people to decide what will be the "look" of the film to be produced. What will be its tone, and how will it be visualized — in other words, how will the film appear in its final form. Exactly to what created images will its target audience relate and respond?

Audience response has been record-breaking for many leading cinematic examples of film's recent digital revolution, including *Pirates of the Caribbean*, the *Lord of the Rings* trilogy, the *Harry Potter* series, *Spiderman*, and *Superman Returns*. These are all digital treasures, live action films that contain awesome, visceral entertainment values that continue to enthrall a world-wide movie audience. They are primary examples of developing *computer graphics imaging (CGI)* and its influence on *special and visual effects (SFX/VFX)*.

All the above cinematic treasures share another primary element that must be noted. Each and every film started not only with the germ of an idea, but also with a small thumbnail sketch — a concept sketch that provided for the production team the visual possibilities of those first written works/descriptions.

**COMPUTER GRAPHICS IMAGING (CGI):** Imagined and executed scenes or elements created on a computer and often combined with live action film.

**SPECIAL AND VISUAL EFFECTS (SFX/VFX):** Interchangeable terms to indicate effects that are not real. These effects can be computer-generated elements or live-action elements shot over a greenscreen.

It can't be stated too many times that the storyboard artist is an integral part of the visualization process, often coming up with concept drawings that illuminate and augment the script narrative. Everyone benefits from the storyboard artist's talent: the director, producer, director of cinematography and the production designer. Often a script starts with a few sentences, a concept or a hook to grab a producer's attention.

With *Pirates of the Caribbean*, producer Jerry Bruckheimer was sold on the fact that *Pirates* wasn't just going to be a film based on a Disneyland ride, but rather a live action film that added the effect of the supernatural to the typical pirate story line. The film was intensely involved with greedy pirate ghosts that appeared human in daylight but became skeletal horrors at night.

Storyboard artists were put to work immediately to visualize for the Disney production team exactly what the lead characters and setting/backgrounds and sets were to look like. The lead characters were drawn in detail then were sculpted by model makers and made into *maquettes* (three-dimensional figures) for all to see. Illustrators, matte painters, model makers (for sets and characters) and concept artists added to the artistic milieu, creating, often by hand, the "look" of the film with their presentation sketches and drawings.

Later, the computer crowd from ILM (Lucas's industrial light and magic) moved in and used CGI to give the narrative its added dimension of supernatural horror. ILM created computer-animated pirates and SFX/VFX. Computer artists gave tremendous graphic adventure to the pirate plot. Casting also played a major role in realizing the final live action film – Disney's biggest selling ever, until topped by the grosses for the second film, *Dead Man's Chest*.

The digital revolution seems to have re-vitalized the film industry. But, you still have to have the initial, individual creative input of the storyboard artist, "hecho a mano" (made by hand). The storyboard artist is the one who makes sense of the initial creative mayhem involved in getting a film produced. The storyboard artist's contribution to the creative team's effort is to help in visually evaluating and synthesizing the narrative flow of the screenplay.

The storyboard artist's job is to give cohesion, interpretation and illustration to the visual spine, the "flux of imagery" that will constitute the screenplay. He or she will render or sketch, when requested by a particular director, all the necessary action in each key sequence or shot. Working with the producer, director, director of photography, and often the production designer, the artist will create a vital blueprint that will be referred to by all of them during the entire shooting schedule of the production and frequently right into the postproduction editing process.

**In a 1998 interview in VISFX with editor Bruce Stockler, Ray Harryhausen responded to a question on how he learned about storyboarding:**

**"I learned storyboarding from Willis O'Brien. He storyboarded everything. He started a film before *King Kong* called *Creation* (1931) at RKO. When Merian Cooper took over, he put the gorilla in it, and they added parts of *Lost World* and they built that up to be *King Kong*. It was a great experience to work with him. He would make 20 or 30 drawings a day, little ones, about the size of the [indicating a napkin] . . . then he would paste them up and write captions underneath and we would do each scene that way. They were all numbered, so you knew when the close-up was coming, the camera angle and the framing, and whether you needed a rear-projector or a split screen or whatever."**

Basically, the same structural techniques were used by Peter Jackson in his 2005 remake of *King Kong*. The big difference being that Jackson's compositing frames set-up (putting as many as 20 or more computer generated images together in one shot) were created especially for Kong by his own company, WETA Digital Effects.

Earlier, WETA Digital had composited such elements as real location shots, matte paintings, 3D miniatures and live actors to create his Oscar winning trilogy *Lord of the Rings* in 2001–2003 (Figure 1-2). *Rings* was followed by *Chronicles of Narnia* (2005) for Disney. Howard Berger, the head creative designer and supervisor for *Chronicles*, relates in the Official Illustrated Movie Companion to *Chronicles of Narnia*, "When I first met [director] Andrew Adamson at his modest office in Burbank, he showed me the presentation room where hundreds of preproduction drawings for the *Narnia* movie hung. These drawings [storyboards] by the preproduction artists

**Figure 1-2 Hart's composite sketch of the characters from Peter Jackson's *Lord of the Rings* trilogy.**

**Figure 1-3 Hart's example of a quick concept sketch drawn on a paper tablecloth in a restaurant. Notice the use of basic geometric shapes and shading.**

**Figure 1-4 This is a structural sketch of the entrance to the anatomical bodies exhibit at the South Street Seaport in Manhattan. Notice the one-point perspective with the vanishing point in the upper righthand corner of the picture.**

were presented in the order of the film as Andrew envisioned it, then we watched his early version of the animatics of the final battle." It seems like old times, because his preproduction artists were following the same pre-visualization procedure Disney introduced 50 or 60 years ago on films like *Snow White and the Seven Dwarfs* and *Song of the South*.

---

## Tutorials

1. Buy a sketchbook and fill each page with drawings of everyday objects. Then work up to sketching people in action – pay attention to the basic geometric construction of any object or figure (Figure 1-3).

2. Purchase a good book on anatomy and study the skeletal and muscular structure of the human body (Figure 1-4). Suggested texts are: *Art Students' Anatomy* by Edmund J. Farris, Dover Books; and *Wall Chart of Human Anatomy* by Thomas McCracken, Anatographica LLC.

3. Compare the original *King Kong* (1933) to Jackson's 2005 version. Make basic structural sketches of key scenes for comparison.

# Chapter 2

## The Storyboard Artist Is Part of the Preproduction Team

Ben Wooten, the conceptual artist and production designer for *Lord of the Rings*, says that "Better design work is done when we all work together swapping ideas. That makes it far more realistic and far more successful. No one works in a vacuum." In short, everyone is a member of a vital creative team, all working toward one major goal: producing a viable yet commercially successful film product. The storyboard artist starts in collaboration with the producer, the director, the production designer/art director and even the lighting designer. *Pre-visualization* is the new catch phrase, and the storyboard artist is the main interpreter of that concept.

Beginning with the *concept sketch* that visualizes a selected scene from a script narrative or making on-the-spot *thumbnail sketches* for the preproduction team, the storyboard artists not only impress those involved but also realize that it is a rewarding creative experience. They note the pleased expressions of the directors and producers when they see the scene created for them visually as the movie takes shape "before their very eyes." Now they have actual images that have come alive, springing up from the script's printed word and translated into reality by the storyboard artist. The art director and the production designer will also relate to the storyboard artists "on demand" output.

PRE-VISUALIZATION (PRE-VIZ): It is the drawings of the storyboard artist that illustrate the visuals that will make up the narrative of the film.

From the beginning, the evolution of the storyboard is intertwined with the history of 20th century cinema. Some directors like Sergei Eisenstein made simple sketches in the margin of the script (Figure 2-1).

Other directors probably kept them in their heads, like John Ford or Cecil B. DeMille in the silent film period. It's my guess that if the early master directors didn't use a storyboard per se; creative visionaries like D. W. Griffith, Eric von Stroheim, Charlie Chaplin and Buster Keaton were very involved in preproduction planning, even if it was simply the basics. For instance, the day and time of specific shoots, which actors were involved, what location, what sets would have to be built, what style costumes would be worn, who would run the cameras, and what scenes were the director and the cameraman going to shoot at what designated time and location?

Some form of preproduction concept sketching is evolved, if only to give the construction and technical crews as well as the actors some idea of what the next shot was going to be. It's unlikely that someone like Griffith, who was shooting 72

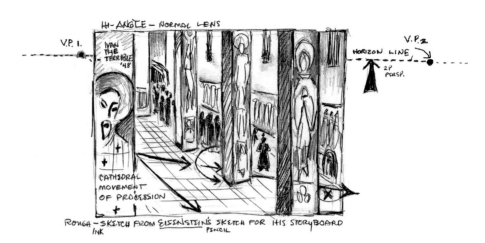

**Figure 2-1 Hart's schematic interpretation of the original Sergei Eisenstein sketch for *Ivan the Terrible, Part II* (1958).**

one- or two-reelers a year, would have had the time to make detailed sketches of every scheduled scene (Figure 2-2).

Although the storyboard was developed in its more sophisticated form by Disney in the 1930s, Griffith certainly preplanned the setups, set construction, camera movements, crane shots and so on. He rehearsed the actors to block each shot. Later, in *Gone with the Wind* (1939), David O. Selznick applied many of Disney's preplanning animation techniques to his Civil War epic.

Frederico Fellini (*La Strada*, 1954; *La Dolce Vita*, 1960; *8½*, 1963) was known to arrive on the set early in the morning and – like Griffith – keep scores of carpenters, actors and technicians waiting around while he worked out in his head where and how the next shot was going to be accomplished. (No one could get away with that now with the multi-million budgets of some productions!) No doubt he spent many hours with his technical people preplanning the use of the expensive sets, the lighting and the camera positions that were needed for his brilliantly imaged film like *La Dolce Vita* or his *8½* (Figure 2-3).

Preplanning for these films? Most certainly. The gigantic budgets demanded it. Storyboarding for action sequences? Probably drawings of concept sketches aligned with the script.

Orson Welles, who worked under even tighter studio controls and budgets with his legendary *Citizen Kane* and *Touch of Evil*, worked out all his key scenes in close collaboration with his award-winning cinematographer Gregg Toland. They story-

**Figure 2-2 Hart sketch of the D. W. Griffith film *Intolerance* (1916). This shot, of one of the largest sets ever built in Hollywood, was taken from a hot air balloon.**

boarded each key frame, especially those scenes involving cast members and extras. They utilized high contrast and ominous shadows that frame the shot (Figure 2-4).

Even as far as budgeting time was concerned, Welles' contemporaries like John Ford, DeMille, Victor Fleming and William Wyler (*The Best Years of Our Lives*, 1947) were all aware that selected storyboards could help realize the "look" of the film, indicate an actor's movements and give the positions of cameras and lighting set-ups implementing the set designer's constructions. Frank Capra (*It's a Wonderful Life*, 1946) made the salient point that "to lower the odds against a film being 'quality,' there is no substitute for intensive attention to preproduction." Ideally, each production element would be worked out ahead of time and dealt with in the consideration of each shot, right up to the final "cut and print it."

In Russia, the great, innovative Eisenstein made a smooth transition from silent movies in the 1920s to the sound films of the 30s and 40s. Eisenstein was a talented and professionally trained artist (like Alfred Hitchcock) who became a theatrical set

CONCEPT SKETCH

**Figure 2-3 Hart sketch of the tower scene from Frederico Fellini's 8½, his autobiographical masterpiece released in 1963.**

**Figure 2-4 Hart sketch of Orson Welles come-back crime drama *A Touch of Evil*
(1958).**

designer before he got into film. Eisenstein designed all the sets and costumes for all his films. Although his classic *Battleship Potemkin* (1925) was shot almost entirely at the actual historical locations depicted in the film, his later works, like *Alexander Nevsky* (1938) and the two-part *Ivan the Terrible* (1945 and 1958), required massive sets built to satisfy the needs of the individual story lines (Figure 2-5).

**Figure 2-5 Hart interpretive sketch of Eisenstein's *Ivan the Terrible II* (1958).**

Many preliminary sketches were made to show not only the settings themselves but also the action and movements of the actors (again, working closely with his brilliant cameraman, Eduard Tisse. It is safe to say that Eisenstein was one of the early directors or auteurs employing rudimentary visual techniques that would later be incorporated into storyboard construction (Figure 2-6).

We have seen the contributions of early animators such as Winsor McKay, who perfected the storyboard technique along with Walt Disney's Ub Iwerks. Disney insisted that his dream factory use the cartoon-style storyboard process. Disney's studio's perfection of animated cartoons is legendary, as are Walt Disney's pioneering efforts (along with Max Fleischer and his Betty Boop cartoons and others in the early 30s) in bringing about many innovations and techniques to which the development of current storyboard styles owe their existence.

Disney and his conceptual artists refined the use of the storyboard as the essential method of pre-visualizing the story to be told (Figure 2-7). It was done first with rough concept sketches, then workbook sketches in color, then sequential animation renderings and finally painting the approved production cels. All the creative personnel knew exactly how each sequence would pertain to the overall story line, which in itself contained "the essential composition of shots and sequences" (Culhane, 1983).

Storyboarding was an absolute necessity due to the thousands of individual cels that had to fill 24 frames per second on 35 mm film and eventually had to be hand-colored. These demanded much greater care than the average film in preparing and painting the separate cels or frames that constituted shots that unified the continuity of the storyboard process. Today all of that is done digitally (CGI).

When the perfectionist producer David O. Selznick was faced with the intimidating task of filming the 1,200-page best-seller *Gone with the Wind*, he insisted on careful preplanning and storyboarding every major scene to be shot in the four-hour film (this Technicolor spectacle was the most expensive movie ever made to that point). The experience his production team had gained previously in the use of special effects on *King Kong* (1933) came in very handy in preparation for the extensive use of matte paintings and composite photography that *Gone with the Wind* demanded.

Selznick hired the most expensive actors in the movie business (like Clark Gable as Rhett Butler) and employed the top designers and technical personnel available in Hollywood. Heading the list of this creative pool, along with the director Victor Fleming (*The Wizard of Oz*, 1939), was the eminent production designer, William Cameron Menzies. Menzies designed the "look" of each key scene and even indicated the camera angles and framing of each shot. He received an Academy Award for his production design. Lyle Wheeler as art director (set designer) and Lee Garmes as the director of photography (Figure 2-8) followed the bidding of the production designers and the directors, creating stunning lighting for the film (Figure 2-9).

**Figure 2-6 Hart original storyboard construction/schematic (six frames) illustrating concepts involved in pre-viz of the script.**

**Figure 2-7 Walt Disney and staff. Storyboards occupy the entire studio wall directly behind them, showing the complete narrative flow of the project.**

**Figure 2-8 Hart sketch of Lyle Wheeler and William Cameron Menzies approving the storyboard production sketches of *Gone with the Wind*.**

**Figure 2-9 Hart interpretive sketch of the burning of Atlanta from *Gone with the Wind*.**

Since the storyboard is concerned with illustrating the flow of action in each key scene, it basically deals with the movement of the actors performing in front of the previously designed sets and lighting. observe the art direction and production design that contribute to the stunning visual presentation of the following films: Ernst Lubitsch's *Ninotchka* (1939); Orson Welles' *Citizen Kane* (1941); David Lean's *Lawrence of Arabia* (1962); Victor Fleming's *Wizard of Oz* and *Gone with the Wind* (both 1939); Alfred Hitchcock's *Rear Window* (1954); Steven Spielberg's *Jaws* (1975), *Indiana Jones and the Temple of Doom* (1984), and *Jurassic Park* (1994); Ridley Scott's *Gladiator* (2001); and Disney's *Pirates of the Caribbean* (2005) and *Pirates of the Caribbean II, Dead Man's Chest* (2006).

Selznick's legendary meticulous attention to detail, covering all facets of the production process, especially preproduction, would pay off handsomely with a shelf-load of Oscars garnered for the biggest grossing hit in Hollywood history. (I saw the re-issued restored color version and it's better than ever.)

One salient point can be made: Many great producers and directors in the history of the motion picture used some form of preproduction planning. They realized how much time and money could be saved (balancing their budgets) if their preproduction people utilized a carefully laid out storyboard that was the "visual spine" of the screenplay. In other words, they could readily see, by referring to storyboard sketches, who had to spend what and for what purpose.

Director John Ford, who supposedly kept the continuity of his shots all in his head, received valuable visual support from several great art directors, including James Basevi. We can marvel at Basevi's brilliantly conceived compositions in *The Grapes of Wrath* (1940), *My Darling Clementine* (1946) and *The Searchers* (1956).

In observing many of the illustration or stills in this book, you will see that each frame of the storyboard creates its own world. It requires the use of design, perspective, mood and *mise-en-scene*. Whether the film is a comedy, tragedy or melodrama, great film directors can create a very spatial world, populated with interesting in-depth characters who, by the force of a dynamic plotline, reward us with great visual entertainment.

For those who have seen them, certain realms of experience have been indelibly imprinted on our memories by the graphic images Alfred Hitchcock created for his films (Figure 2-10). He was responsible for such hair-raisers as *Psycho* (1960), *The Birds* (1963) and *North by Northwest* (1959).

Each shot of these movies was filled with stunning imagery and visual impact. Each was designed to flow with the narrative of the screenplay. Hitchcock made exciting use of the montage concepts culled from Eisenstein, Griffith and Chaplin and imprinted them with his own suspense-oriented style.

Hitchcock was a major proponent of storyboarding for every one of his productions. In many of his movies, like *The Birds*, elaborate special effects that involved

MISE-EN-SCENE: placement of actors within a given scene, simply tells us visually where the action takes place.

**Figure 2-10 Hart interpretative drawing of an explosive shot from Hitchcock's *North by Northwest*. The theme of the mistaken identity had been used by Hitchcock in *The 39 Steps*, *The Man Who Knew Too Much* and *The Wrong Man*.**

composite shots of live action sequences combined with matte paintings and blue-screens made the execution of storyboards imperative (Figure 2-11).

Hitchcock (like Eisenstein) was a prolific director whose career spanned silent films to sound and continued to his last film, *Family Plot,* in 1976. From an advertising layout man in a London Department store to art director for *Woman to Woman* in 1923 to full-fledged director of *The Lodger* in 1926, "his background in advertising layout was to help him in his directorial duties. In planning each film, he would make hundreds of sketches (storyboards) illustrating the camera angles and the facial expressions he wanted from the main characters" (Spoto, 1976).

More recent films have given us creative blasts from outer space like the George Lucas movies. The storyboarding of his *Star Wars* trilogy coordinated and imple-

**Figure 2-11 A recent example of an eye-catching storyboard by Eric de Jong, 2006, www.erikdejong.eu, www.illustrationen.de. It has great graphics and dynamic close-ups and illustrates the use of camera angles, horizontals and verticals, and gives the indication of special effects.**

mented all of the composite shots that involved actors, space craft, animated miniatures, matte drawing and other special effects, many of which were conceived by master storyboard painter Ralph McQuarrie.

Industrial light and magic (ILM), founded by Lucas to handle in-house special effects of his films, later worked with other directors and producers creating more SFX magic in Steven Spielberg's *Jurassic Park* (1994); Jan De Bont's *Twister* (1996); and the potboiler trilogy *Mission Impossible* (1996), *Mission Impossible II* (2000) and *Mission Impossible III* (2006). James Cameron's memorable *Titanic* had some of the most stunning visual effects of the 90s. Another Cameron film, *Terminator 2* (1991), was considered ahead of its time, using morphing (digitally changing one form into another) with dynamic effect.

*Twister* is replete with heart-pounding, visceral SFXs created by the innovative ILM team. All those nonstop tornado thrills in *Twister* were storyboarded beforehand so that not only De Bont, but also the producer, art director, director of photography and the entire string of technicians could consult the storyboards during the entire shooting schedule. De Bont said, "You have to make storyboards, and the storyboards have to explain to every department exactly what is demanded of them" (Weiner, May 1996).

Stunning visuals are also seen in the recent *Da Vinci Code* (2006) (Figure 2-12), *Casino Royale* (2006) and *Spiderman II* (2007).

ILM (now in competition with WETA and DreamWorks Digital) has been busy doing special effects for the commercial markets that — because of its own tight budgets and time scheduling of talent and equipment — demands the use of a detailed storyboard. The art of the storyboard, with all of its techniques and adaptations, has been tailored to the requirements of the divergent needs of commercials, industrial films, music videos, computer animation and other productions (Figure 2-13).

However, there is nothing new to this. Disney animators were doing this in Chicago for commercials and industrials in 1971.

Renaissance architect Leone Battista Alberti, writing circa 1470 in Florence, said: "The architect must know exactly what to do before construction can begin [script concept]. The building must already be fully complete in his mind [pre-viz, like Hitchcock or Peter Jackson]. He must have made drawings [storyboard artist] and scale models complete in every detail, including the sculptural decoration [production designer], so that he can estimate costs [producer], prepare his materials [CGI and VFX] and workforce, and bring them to the building site [sets and lighting]."

Anyone attempting to shoot any kind of story line, even the harried film student or independent filmmaker doing their first documentary, should use the storyboard as a visual device. It serves not only as a day-to-day guide for setting up shots (with

**Figure 2-12 Hart composite schematic of Ron Howard's *Da Vinci Code*, a murky retelling of the book of the same name. It's best known for its production design, scale models and SFX.**

**Figure 2-13 A storyboard by Eric de Jong, 2006, www.erikdejong.eu, www.illustrationen.de. Note the delineation of the car and wolf, its naturalness, the composition/design of each frame, and his imaginative use of camera angles.**

their inherent problems of lighting, blocking and pace), but also as a precious time-saver and aid in controlling budgets of any size.

A case in point was Gregory La Cava (*Stage Door*, 1937; *My Man Godfrey*, 1936). In his autobiography, *The Name Above the Title*, Frank Capra described La Cava as a very witty director, who was guilty of "inventing scenes on the set." La Cava had proclaimed that "he could make motion pictures without scripts," but without scripts, the studio heads could not make accurate budgets, schedules or time allowance for actors' commitments. "Shooting off the cuff," executives said, "was reckless gambling; film costs would be open-ended and no major company could afford such risks." Capra goes on to tell us that La Cava's meteoric rise was followed by a very sad fall because of his lack of preproduction planning.

In contrast, Capra described the legendary director Ernst Lubitsch (who directed Greta Garbo in *Ninotchka*, 1939) as "the complete architect of his films." His scripts were detailed blueprints, replete with all the required sketches, drawings and specifications. Every scene, every look, every camera angle was designed in advance of photography and he seldom, if ever, deviated from blueprints in the actual shooting. "His stamp was on every frame of film from conception to delivery."

Another case for good preproduction planning is Terry Gilliam's *The Adventures of Baron Munchausen* (1988). In "Losing the Light" (Yule, 1991), actor Charles McKeown was quoted as saying, "If you start a movie unprepared, you never catch up. You lose morale and there's an instant sense of failure, no matter how hard everyone works. On *Munchausen*, nothing was ready, nothing was right." Missed deadlines, escalating budgets and problems with communication damaged the collaborative effort and jeopardized the film. Apparently, the storyboards were one saving factor. Gilliam is quoted as saying, "It might not be in the script, but you'll find it on the storyboards." The actor said, "If you took your eye off a combination of the script and the storyboards on this incredibly complicated film even for one minute, you were lost."

The value of good preproduction planning and storyboarding as a part of that process cannot be overstressed. Consider what cinematographer Hiro Jarita, ASC, said of director Henry Selick while they were collaborating on the technically demanding live/animation film, *James and the Giant Peach*, 1997 (Figure 2-14).

"I pre-programmed each of the different lighting situations. That way I could go from a day shoot to a night shoot in 29 minutes. That forced us to do a lot of pre-rigging." (Blair, June 1996) Fortunately, Selick had done a great deal of storyboarding.

As illustrated in Figure 2-6, the art of the storyboard is a controlled art, a sequential art – an art form concerned with the illustration or depiction of a given story line with one specific end in mind, the realization of these kinetic drawings in filmic terms.

EX. FORCED/COMPRESSED PERSPECTIVE

**Figure 2-14 Hart sketch of *James and the Giant Peach*. This visual treat of the classic children's tale, by Roald Dahl, was directed by Henry Selick. Notice the use of forced perspective. The house in the BKD is only 10″ high. The center of interest (giant peach) is placed off-center in the upper lefthand corner.**

The storyboard represents the line of dynamic movement dictated by a given script that has been chosen for production.

Based on basic comic strip art forms, the storyboard is, in effect, a shot-by-shot visual programming of the suggested action of the script and as such dictates its own artistic requirements. It must demonstrate graphic visualizations for the producer, director, director of photography and the director of special effects. Consider the growing sophistication and phenomenal costs of SFX exploding in earlier productions like Spielberg's *The War of the Worlds* (2005), which was budgeted at about $100 million, up to the present day movies with truly spectacular special effects like Guillermo Del Toro's *Pan's Labyrinth* (2007) called a "tour de force of cinematic imagination" by the *New York Times*, Disney's fantasy *Bridge to Terabithia* (2007) and Joel Schumacher's scary thriller *The Number 23* (2007). Suffice to say, this increased reliance on SFX makes demands on the storyboard artist and his or her imagination even more acute and more challenging. Naturally, any visual effects will be indicated in the storyboard sequence.

The storyboard then is broken up into flowing action that emanates from each pre-planned shot. Since the shot is the heart of every image set up, it contains its own dynamic. Its primary purpose, illustrated in the storyboard, is to realize the kinetic intentions of each dramatic section of the script, giving specific assistance to the director in capturing his or her personal vision. The individual shot implies more than it suggests, since each shot is the keystone of every scene in the script. The inherent essence of the phrase, *the shot* will be discussed at length in later chapters.

In *Birth of a Nation* (1915) and particularly in *Intolerance* (1916), D. W. Griffith developed editing and montage techniques that, along with his creation of the close-up, iris, pans and tilts, became the foundation of film grammar and in turn, influenced worldwide film direction, particularly and dramatically for Sergei Eisenstein in Russia.

Although Eisenstein is justly a legendary figure for the filmic strength of *Strike* (1925), *Alexander Nevsky* and *Ivan the Terrible, Parts I* and *II*, he is most remembered for the absolute graphic power of his Odessa Steps sequence from *Battleship Potemkin*. This memorable action sequence can serve as the premiere "catechism" and learning tool for the student of storyboarding. This brief background of the beginnings of the storyboard and its use by the "greats" is explored later in greater detail.

To repeat the key point of this chapter, storyboard artists produce pre-viz formats in collaboration with the director and preproduction team, which are the springboard for the superb visuals shown to audiences worldwide.

---

## Tutorials

1. After seeing some of the films discussed in this chapter, compare on paper the visual effects of the old with the new. You'll begin to see how the storyboard is actually used.

2. Pick a short scene from a recent film and create your own storyboard for that scene.

3. During credit rolls, note the name of the storyboard artist, look up the credits and check out his or her style.

4. Do the same for the composite or VFX artist(s).

# **Chapter 3**

## The Storyboard Artist and the Storyboard

One of the biggest challenges facing the storyboard artist is the demands of the various members of the preproduction team. Trying to satisfy the visual and narrative requirements of the script as interpreted by the producer, director, director of photography, cinematographer, art director, production designer, set designer and the SFX team is a formidable task.

As a storyboard artist, you must be ready to create on demand and to deliver professional quality sketches under pressure. You must have a thorough knowledge of design and drawing, particularly the human figure in motion. This book will give you a jump-start toward a basic knowledge of design and drawing skills. The rest is up to you. "How do you get to Carnegie Hall?" a New York cab driver was asked. He replied, "Practice, practice, practice!"

Director Ronald Petrie (*Mystic Pizza*, 1988), when interviewed on IFC, said there are nine important words to remember when approaching any new project. His nine "P's" are: "Prodigious Preproduction Planning Prevents Piss-Poor Postproduction." He's right on and as a functioning storyboard artist you are an essential component of that preproduction planning process.

### THE DIRECTOR'S VISION

With storyboards, the producer can make a much better estimate of costs and therefore develop a realistic budget. The director uses the storyboards for shot sequences, blocking the actors, camera setups and lighting.

David O. Selznick, the king of producers, went over every storyboard sequence executed for *Gone with the Wind* with his production designer William Cameron Menzies and with art director/set designer Lyle Wheeler. They were able to give the movie a visual consistency that survived the film's three directors, Sam Wood, George Cukor and Victor Fleming. They were able to maintain the look of this epic through all the changes in part because of the preproduction sketches and storyboards.

The director ideally first goes over the storyboards with the director of photography, who will use appropriate visual concepts drawn from hundreds of shot sequences to decide which cameras to rent, what lenses are needed, what film stock and what lighting design will best create the right atmosphere or look of the picture (Figure 3-1). Since SFX have become such an important part of so many films today, the producer, director, cinematographer and production designer will want to see the storyboard visuals that illustrate any SFX. The storyboards are used to figure costs and to set up shots, lighting and framing, as well as design sets in conjunction with model builders, miniature makers and greenscreen technicians and so on.

In 1939, the production cost of *Gone with the Wind* was in excess of $6 million. In 1999, Titanic cost $200 million. I shudder to think what it cost for the bookish young stepdaughter of a sadistic army general to escape into the eerie fantasy world of *Pan's Labyrinth* in 2006. Any producer, faced with the daunting assignment of developing a budget for today's films, needs all the help available, and storyboards can be an effective tool for this all important preproduction work.

The visuals offered by the storyboard are especially important to illustrate SFX when the storyboard artist works with the producer, director, cinematographer and production designer, then makes whatever changes become necessary in order to accommodate their vision or "look" of the script relating to SFX.

**Figure 3-1 A scene from *Kingdom of Heaven* (2005), an action/adventure period piece, showing the placement of the multi-directional camera and boom used for the shot.**

**The *Dictionary of Television and Film* has a great definition of SFX: "Any visual action, image or effect that cannot be obtained with the camera shooting in normal operation directly at the action and which requires prearranged special techniques of apparatus added to the camera, action, processing or editing. Special effects include contour matting; multiple image montages, split screens, and vignetting; animation; use of models or miniatures; special props such as break-away glass and furniture; simulated bullet wounds, injuries, explosions, floods, fires; and any mechanical or visual effect whether created on location, in the lab during processing, or in editing in postproduction."**

A current example of SFX is the storyboard frame in Figure 3-2, a production sketch drawn for a Duncan Film venture whose working title is *The Fu Project*. It tells the story of a Chinese astronaut whose space capsule falls to Earth and is discovered by a young Chinese girl. Here, the space agency helicopters are lifting the capsule's parachute up and off of the trees where the astronaut has landed. Also in this shot, he is pointing to the rush of journalists advancing toward them from frame right.

**Figure 3-2 Enlarged storyboard frame with indications for a composite shot including actors, scenery and CGI of the helicopter.**

Directional arrows indicate the two lead characters, the hordes of media, and the upward direction of the parachute being lifted. SFX or VFX indications in this enlarged storyboard frame would include requests for hi-definition imagery, for a composite shot which would include the human elements, the actual forest locale, and CGI of the helicopter's action.

In the space below the framed storyboard, detailed instructions should be made, not only indicating the action movements, but also any SFX that are needed in the final shooting script so the production isn't flying blind. With SFX, as with everything else, it's the concept that counts and storyboards are the process that renders that concept. For example, as I watched the 20<sup>th</sup> anniversary screening of *Star Wars*, it occurred to me that the jaw-dropping SFX of this ultimate science fiction film were, in part, a result of the creative imagination of Ralph McQuarrie. Ralph did the conceptual storyboards (some the size of a postage stamp) for ILM and also rendered finished production paintings illustrating Darth Vader's mask, Storm Trooper uniforms, and the awe inspiring sets for the Rebel Ceremony, the interior of the Death Star and the Death Star trench. Ralph was ably assisted by Peter Ellenshaw, a legendary matte painting artist, who did most of the background scenes in the composite shots. New storyboarding was done for the computer generated characters like Jabba the Hut for the anniversary release. (Get the definitive book on the subject, Titelman's profusely illustrated *The Art of Star Wars*.)

Jean Cocteau directed *Beauty and the Beast* (*La Belle et la Bete*) during the last days of the German occupation of France in 1945. This is an example of the film as a collaborative art form at its most challenging. Cocteau's filming style was derived from his association with the surrealist movement in the late 20s and 30s. This fantasy film has been described as the most beautiful black-and-white movie ever made. For me, this *Beauty* is much better than the Disney version from 1991. Jean Marais starred in Cocteau's film as the frighteningly imposing Beast (Figure 3-3) whose chateau – with its surrealistic environment – evokes dreamlike movements and strange situations that confound Beauty.

For example, the idea of Beauty entering the Beast's hallway and seeing candelabras being held by human arms (Figure 3-4) is a stunning visual concept adapted by the Disney animators in their 1991 feature film. The arrow at the base of the frame indicates Beauty's floating movement toward the camera.

It was the collaborative effort of the entire production team that enabled this movie to be produced, directed and shot under the most trying of circumstances. Cocteau's uncanny imagination, aided by the artists who put his ideas on paper, produced dazzling SFX without a single computer in sight. Understanding the surrealist visual demands of this fantasy/fairy tale, he conjured up his own magical kingdom with filmic slight of hand. Interpreting the visual field as a symbolic dreamscape is evident in all of Cocteau's films, starting with *Blood of the Poet* (1930) and culminating with his very surrealistic *Orphee* (1950). All of Cocteau's films are a viewing must.

**Figure 3-3 The ugly Beast – with sad eyes and the dress and manners of a 17ᵗʰ century gentleman – and Beauty – who is both intimidated and intrigued.**

Terry Gilliam's fanciful *The Adventures of Baron Munchausen* (1989) is another piece of brilliant art direction and set design (by Martin Scorcese's favorite production designer, Dante Ferretti) blended with bold SFX to produce an adventure/comedy/fantasy which recounts the Baron's fantastical experiences with his band of misfits. The storyboarding for this film, many by the director, included dozens of sketches of props and scenery in addition to the VFX and normal shots (Figure 3-5).

Figure 3-4 Hart sketch of scene from *Beauty and the Beast*, an example of one-point perspective.

Figure 3-5 An example of one-point perspective and an elaborate prop. The bed was called *King of the Moons*.

Steven Frears' 2006 biography/drama *The Queen* begins after the untimely death of Diana, Princess of Wales. Prime Minister Tony Blair must defuse the bad public relations situation caused by Queen Elizabeth's restrained reaction. It is always difficult to create a film about a living person and to do so with some accuracy. Storyboarding the scenes becomes especially important so shots are crafted in a way that allows the director to give the precise motivation needed for the actors, along with the exact camera angles and the lighting plots to produce the desired effect for a given scene. Though these technical areas are important in all films, even when dealing with a film that uses little or no SFX, the entire weight of the film is not only on the actors, but also on the feel or "look" that that film has evoked from the storyboards and pre-viz (Figure 3-6).

At the other end of the film reality spectrum is *The Chronicles of Narnia: The Lion, the Witch and the Wardrobe* (2005) which would not have been the spectacular film it is without the SFX that dominated the movie. An action, adventure and drama for the whole family, it's about four kids who travel through a wardrobe to the land of Narnia. They must defeat the Witch, and to do so they join forces with Aslan, a

**Figure 3-6 *The Queen* is posing for her coronation painting. "Tradition prepared her, change will define her." In this frame, the composition has been carefully balanced with the figure of the Queen placed in the left of the frame, balanced by the artist in the right of the frame.**

mystical lion god. It is their destiny to free Narnia and a great battle ensues between good and evil. Director Andrew Adamson coordinated a huge cast, most of whom were in fanciful makeup and costumes. Without the talent of storyboard artists, without the availability of the storyboards showing the shot-by-shot sequence of this complicated production, I don't think this spectacular film would have been produced (Figure 3-7).

**Figure 3-7 Hart interpretative sketch of the opposing forces of good – Aslan, the lion god – and evil – the Witch.**

Akira Kurosawa's *Rashomon* hit the international film community in 1950 like a flash of sunlight off a samurai's sword. This is a vibrantly kinetic film starring Toshiro Mifune as Tajōmaru, a medieval bandit on trial for murder. His story is related by three different witnesses, each telling a different version of the grisly incident. The film is filled with dazzling production designs coupled with the styling of Kabuki Theater and Japanese scroll paintings. From its brilliant opening sequence in a ruined, rain-swept temple to its conclusion in the same temple, you can't take your eyes off the screen. In Figure 3-8, Tajōmaru is being interrogated by the judge. Any storyboard artist would be thrilled to have worked with Kurosawa THE master of visual dynamics exemplified in such internationally acclaimed films as *Throne of Blood*, and *The Seven Samurai*.

The ideal situation in film production is to work like a family, with every member of the creative force working together to achieve a final product. Producers and directors realize that the best scenario is to have all the creative departments working as a smooth, well-oiled creative machine, with each member of the production staff endeavoring to satisfy the narrative and visual demands of the script. Most of the names that roll by in the film credits belong to people behind the scenes. Though

**Figure 3-8 Hart interpretative sketch of *Rashomon* during the judge's interrogation of Tajōmaru, defiantly retelling his version of the rape and murder.**

ego certainly has its place in the artistic environment of a film production – all of us need to feel secure in our professions – it is important to remember that there is room for everyone's inspirations.

As a storyboard artist you have to be a good listener, always considering other artist's points of view. Above all keep a good sense of humor, after all, sporting a jocular positive attitude will help achieve the common goal – finishing the film.

## Tutorials

1. Analytically look at a film from the standpoint of producer, director, director of photography and production designer. Tell the story as each character requests, then work as the storyboard artist to make rough concept sketches for each member of the team. Take into consideration the various visual demands of each.

2. Pick three key scenes from a screenplay of your choice and make quick rough sketches of each scene, with an imaginative, and, hopefully, original eye to the needs of the production.

# Chapter 4

## Basic Components and Principles of the Storyboard

Steven Spielberg's storyboard sketches for *Indiana Jones and the Temple of Doom* are little more than chicken scratches, but since his concepts for the action sequences were at least indicated, even primitively, he was able to visually convey his ideas to a professional storyboard artist who, in turn, rendered them in a storyboard that was then used by the whole preproduction staff.

In drawing the basic components of the storyboard, all of the design principles discussed here have but one goal: to reproduce and augment the exterior 3D reality on a 2D surface – the movie screen. Even with the current digital revolution, the weapon of choice for pre-viz of the working film script is still pencil on paper. Drawn storyboards rendered within the parameters of the script's narrative structure should be as graphically dynamic as possible. Why? Because the audience's visual interest must be engaged and maintained.

### RULE OF THIRDS

Just as a writer has to face a blank page, the artist has to face a blank rectangle on a drawing pad and visualize how to fill that space with the demands of the script. But even before we fill it, the space itself must be in good proportion. Storyboards are drawn in elongated rectangles, to match the aspect ratio of the final image. The aspect ratio of the projected image can range from 1.65 : 1 to 2.55 : 1 in today's wide screen formats. These are the same proportions the storyboard artist would use to draw the individual frames. The Greeks called it the *divine proportion* or the *golden rectangle*. The base of the Parthenon is two-thirds the total of the building height, and the pediment triangle is the top one-third (Figure 4-1). This division of thirds is a proportional device utilized in the entire history of art.

When constructing divine proportion, start with the square and follow the steps in Figure 4-2 to create a golden rectangle. The "empty" rectangle is the base of any illustration and, like all art, is based on geometric shapes.

Paul Cézanne, the French painter known for beginning the Cubist movement at the turn of the 20th century, stated that all reality is made up of the cone, the sphere and the cylinder (Figure 4-3). *The Raiders of the Lost Ark* sketch in Figure 4-4 demonstrates the design use of Cézanne's observation applied to film design. The sphere

The architects for the Parthenon on the Acropolis (finished in 438 BC), were Ictinus and Callicrates under the supervision of Pericles. "Doric architecture at its zenith, the architects having achieved a perfection of proportion realized neither before nor since" (Emily Cole, "The Grammar of Architecture").

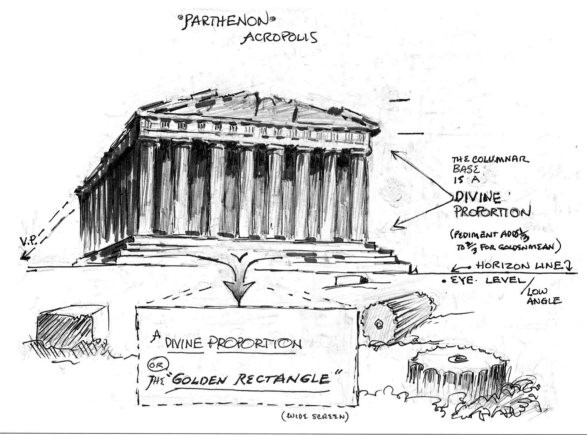

**Figure 4-1 The Parthenon is an example of the divine proportion.**

is obvious; Jones can be a cylinder, cone or a pyramid mass as he moves quickly to the right of the frame.

Any professional composition for any frame of film has to follow these historic artistic principles for correct placement of figures, objects or structures drawn within the storyboard frame. The rectangle must first be divided horizontally and vertically into three sections. The points formed by the intersection of the three verticals and the three horizontals (Figure 4-5) become the areas where the center of interest is always placed. This is called the *rule of thirds*.

The drawing in Figure 4-6 illustrates these points, showing how placement of key elements at the centers of interest frames the shot. The points that are formed by intersecting the three verticals and the three horizontals are the areas where you place the center of interest.

**RULE OF THIRDS:** All framed shots are divided into thirds either (or both) vertically or horizontally, resulting in the placement of the center of action at any of the intersections.

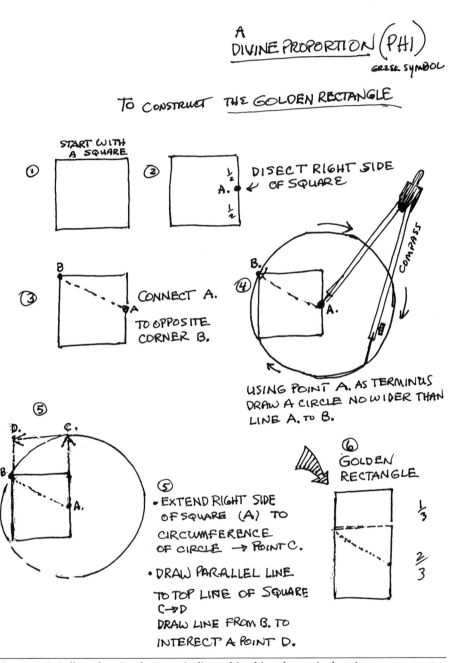

A
DIVINE PROPORTION (PHI)
GREEK SYMBOL

TO CONSTRUCT THE GOLDEN RECTANGLE

① START WITH A SQUARE

② DISECT RIGHT SIDE OF SQUARE
$\frac{1}{2}$
A.
$\frac{1}{2}$

③ CONNECT A. TO OPPOSITE CORNER B.

④ COMPASS
USING POINT A. AS TERMINUS DRAW A CIRCLE NO WIDER THAN LINE A. TO B.

⑤ EXTEND RIGHT SIDE OF SQUARE (A) TO CIRCUMFERENCE OF CIRCLE → POINT C.
• DRAW PARALLEL LINE TO TOP LINE OF SQUARE C→D
DRAW LINE FROM B. TO INTERECT A POINT D.

⑥ GOLDEN RECTANGLE
$\frac{1}{3}$
$\frac{2}{3}$

**Figure 4-2 Follow the simple steps indicated in this schematic drawing to construct a golden rectangle (divine proportion).**

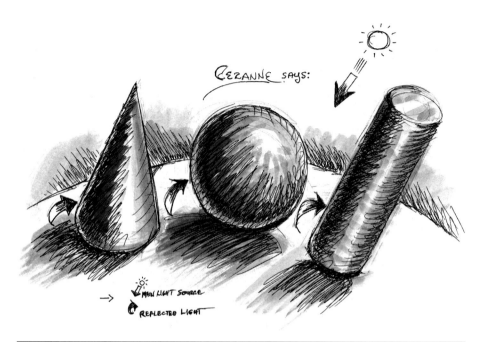

**Figure 4-3 Cézanne believed that everything could be constructed out of just three basic shapes: the cone, sphere and cylinder.**

Another example of concentric circles that frame the center of interest (Figure 4-7) shows a variation on the use of ovals. The eye follows the wingspan of the seagulls, which almost become arrows pointing to the center of interest – the couple in the lower right corner. Figure 4-8 shows nature's example of concentric circles in the conch shell.

This rule of thirds is utilized by all professional storyboard artists and production designers. Centering actors or objects in the exact center of any frame is boring, just as a line that intersects the rectangle in the center of the frame is a mistake. A composition is never split evenly in two. Never. Look at Figure 4-9 and you will see that in a landscape the sky will take up two-thirds of the frame while the land will take up one-third or vice versa, in order to correctly place your center of interest.

## FOREGROUND, MIDDLE GROUND AND BACKGROUND

You will also maintain the visual interest in your storyboards by keeping in mind each of the basic visual planes that constitute perceived reality – the foreground, the middle ground and the background, often abbreviated as FGD, MGD and BGD (Figure 4-10).

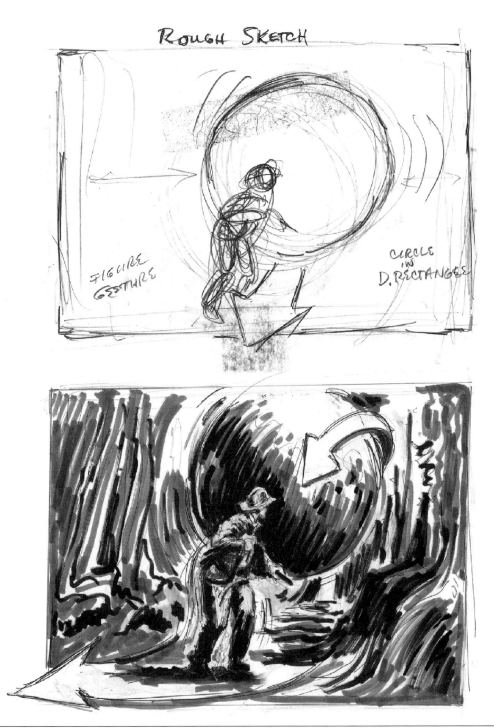

**Figure 4-4 Cézanne's theory applied to a modern-day film.**

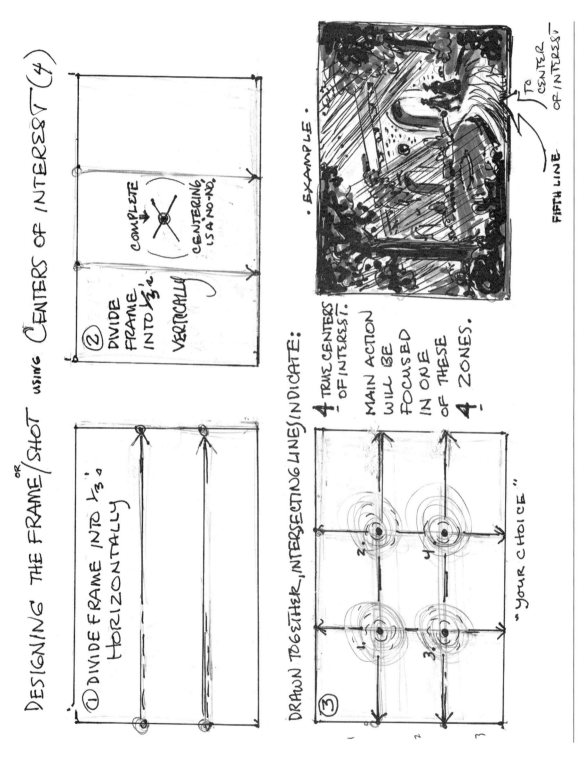

DESIGNING THE FRAME OR SHOT USING CENTERS OF INTEREST (4)

① DIVIDE FRAME INTO ⅓'s HORIZONTALLY

② DIVIDE FRAME INTO ⅓'s VERTICALLY

COMPLETE

CENTERING IS A NO-NO.

③ DRAWN TOGETHER, INTERSECTING LINES INDICATE:

4 TRUE CENTERS OF INTEREST.

MAIN ACTION WILL BE FOCUSED IN ONE OF THESE 4 ZONES.

"YOUR CHOICE"

• EXAMPLE •

TO CENTER OF INTEREST

FIFTH LINE

**Figure 4-5 The rule of thirds identifies the best location for the center of interest in a given shot or frame of film.**

Figure 4-6 The concentric circles created by the path and the trees frame the center of interest.

Figure 4-7 Ovals lead to center of interest.

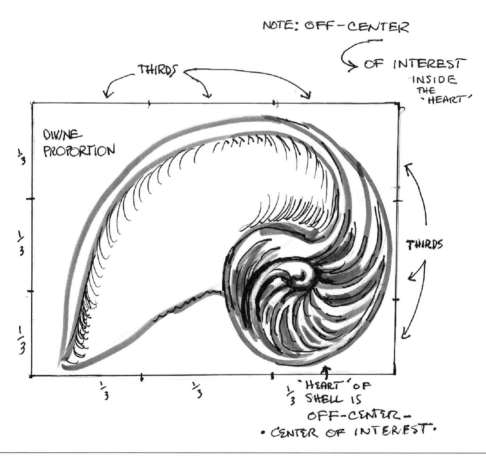

**Figure 4-8 Nature follows the rule of thirds and divine proportion too!**

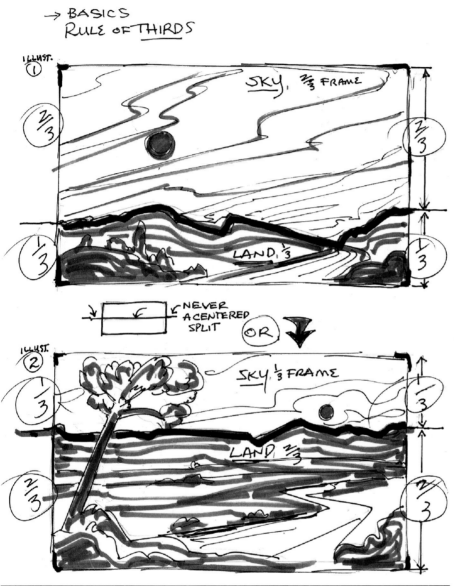

**Figure 4-9 The most compelling compositions will divide the frame in varying proportion (into thirds).**

RECESSION OF PLANES FGD, MDG, BKGD,

LOCATION SHOT

2/3

AN ESTABLISHING SHOT?

AND, OR, MASTER SHOT (HORIZONT- ALLY!)

1/3

BKD →

MDG →

FGD. →

ALSO ATMOSPHERIC PERSPECTIVE

**Figure 4-10 This Hart photograph of Central Park is an example of the rule of thirds and the use of FGD, MGD and BGD. The moving figures in the foreground in the lower third of the picture are our center of interest.**

Figure 4-11 shows a production shot from *Memoirs of a Geisha* where the geisha is framed by the director of photography and the sound man holding the boom mic. The geisha and her friend are centered but moving off-center to exit at the right of the frame. The camera operator and sound man are in the FGD of this image, while the actresses are in the MGD. The BGD sets the scene for the shot, showing

**Figure 4-11 Sketch of *Memoirs of a Geisha* uses FGD, MGD and BGD to convey a rich and interesting scene.**

where it takes place. The sketch also demonstrates concentric circles as a framing device. The movie won Academy Awards for Production Design, Costume Design and Cinematography.

## DEVELOPING DRAWING SKILLS

Once again, the concept of the story line and its validity is what counts in conveying the visual interpretation of a written scene broken down into the individual shots. The director has decided which specific shots are needed to interpret the continuity of the screenplay. Our purpose here is to make you familiar with the storyboard process and help you develop your drawing and drafting skills by actually rendering storyboards. Through this process, I hope, you will develop your own style.

To help you in that direction, let's start out by simply drawing some very basic figures in action (Figure 4-12). It's a must that you carry a sketchbook with you at all times

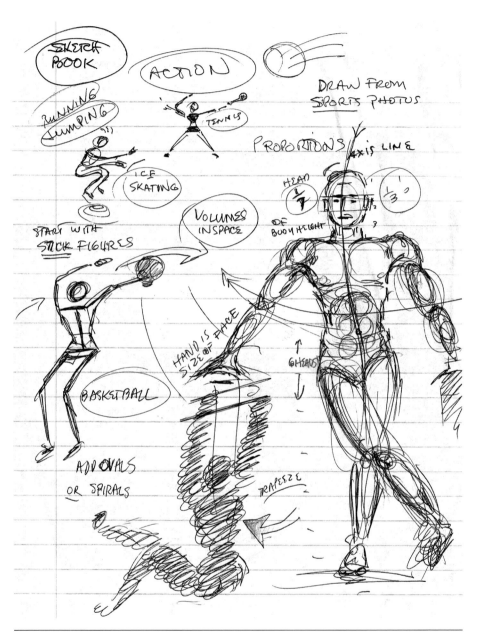

**Figure 4-12 Examples of quick sketches that I have done, many of which were taken right from the TV screen as I watched movies.**

so that you can make quick sketches of the people, places, and objects you encounter every day. This way, through practice, you will develop the facility of rendering figures quickly and naturally.

As you make these sketches, keep in mind the proportions of the body. Try to render your sketches in 15 or 20 seconds. This way, even if they are not perfect, you will at least be getting the "gesture" or direction of the body's movement. Just like a good storyboard, they will have a *line of action*. They will indicate a line of action through their gestures or body stance. The more you sketch, the more you will be developing your own drawing style.

The following sketches are examples of the types of drawing you can execute after your anatomy tutorial in Figure 4-13.

You can start simply with sketching your own hand (Figure 4-14). Enrolling in a local art school to take figure drawing lessons is encouraged. No time? Then work from a wooden model (as on the right of Figure 4-14) or even from figural toys. In Figure 4-15, the young lady ice skating was sketched from a small toy. By simply twisting it, I gave her movement from the left to the right side of the frame. Note the use of division of thirds, medium shots, close-ups and the arrow indications for movement/line of action.

The soldier with a dog (Figure 4-16) and the dancing dog (Figure 4-17) were sketched to show action, while the wedding couple (Figure 4-18) shows a sketch of a high angle shot.

□ ▬ □ ▬ □ ▬ □ ▬
LINE OF ACTION: The gesture of a figure or the continuity of the action itself in the storyboard.

## SHOT ANGLES

One of the most dynamic aspects of cinematography is the ability to change camera angles to present different perspectives, convey different presentations of a scene or show the audience all that you want them to see. Camera angles are a critical way to keep the audience interested in the story you are telling – imagine if you saw only one point of view for an entire movie. It wouldn't be very stimulating.

Therefore, you will likely work closely with the preproduction crew to determine the best angles for each shot and this needs to be accounted for on the storyboard. Throughout the book, you will see reference to a wide variety of shots, so here is a list of the most common ones:

● Close-Up (CU): full face shot of actor(s) or up close shot of objects.

● Extreme Close-Up (EXT CU): so close you see only actor's eyes.

● Establishing Shot (EST): shows the placement of the actor(s) for the audience.

● Long Shot (LS): shows the actor(s) or objects in the distance (background).

● Medium Shot (MS): shows the actor(s) or objects in the MGD.

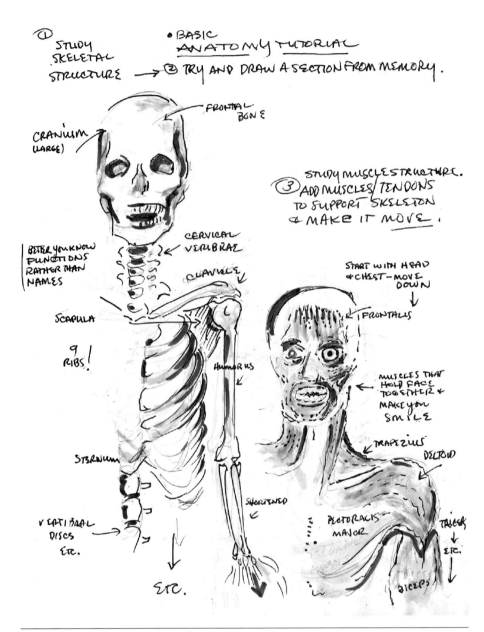

**Figure 4-13 A sketch on skeletal structure.**

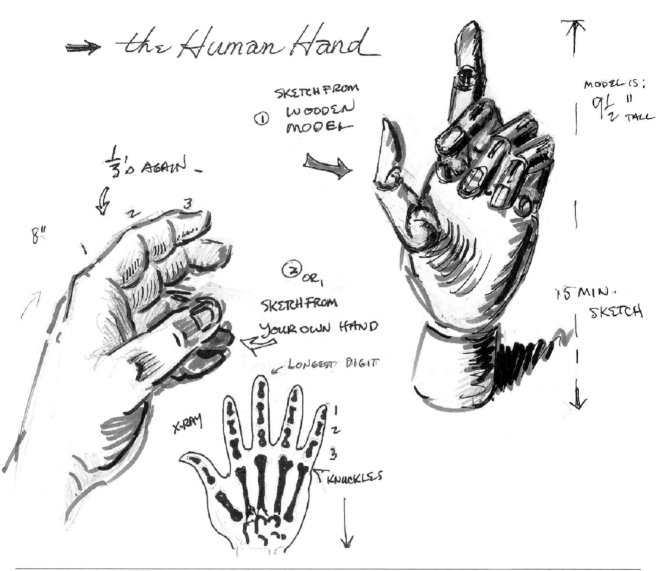

**Figure 4-14 Drawing simple anatomy: my hand, a wooden model and a skeletal rendition.**

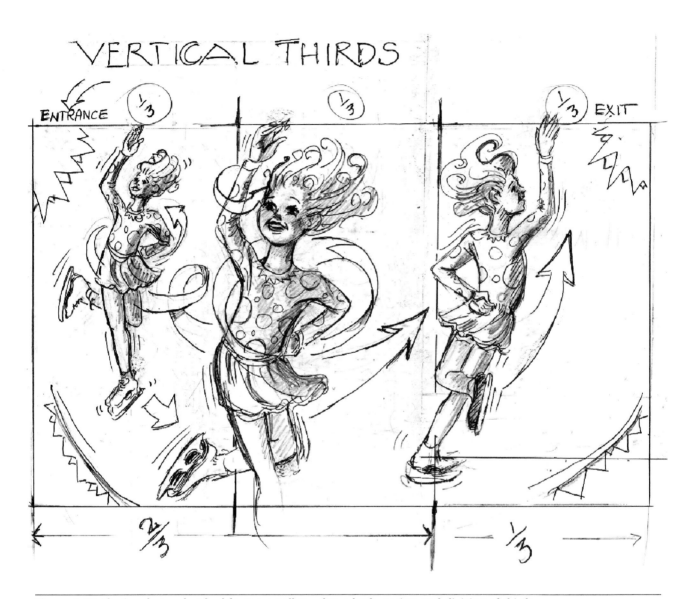

**Figure 4-15 The ice skater sketched from a small toy shows both motion and division of thirds.**

**Figure 4-16 Both the soldier and the dog show the line of action of the shot.**

**Figure 4-17 The fanciful dancing dog shows movement and expression.**

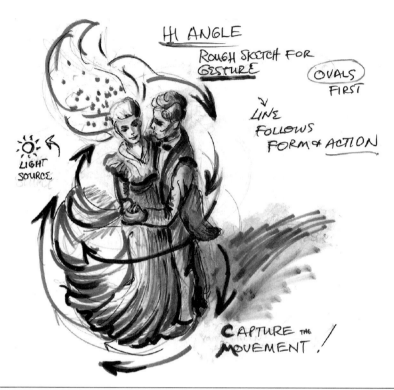

**Figure 4-18 The high angle of the sketch shows the use of concentric circles in the movement of the couple.**

- Over the shoulder (OTS): taken over-the-actors-shoulder; must stay consistent (on same shoulder) for an actor.

- Panoramic (Pan): the camera moves horizontally to take in a panoramic scene.

- Tracking shot: the camera is mounted on wheels and moves smoothly on a track to capture the movement in the scene. Sometimes a similar "dolly" shot is used, where the camera is pulled or pushed on a cart, like the crab dolly that moves in circular motion.

- Zoom shot: the focus goes from wide angle to CU with a zoom lens.

Figure 4-19, from *True Grit* (1969), is a three-shot of John Wayne with his two antagonists framing the FGD. It is an example of an over-the-shoulder shot, in this case, over the shoulders of the two bad guys. Our hero is positioned dead center between then and is lit with the key light aimed directly at him.

Figure 4-20 is a rough sketch I made while watching *Citizen Kane*; it's the scene where Charles Foster Kane in the background is yelling after the politician exiting

**Figure 4-19 John Wayne in *True Grit*.**

to the right of the frame. Arrows indicate the line of action. The camera will frame this flow of action; Welles directed cinematographer Gregg Toland to hold on the low angle shot, to let the politician exit out of the right of the frame. This simple sketch would be enough for a director of photography to follow. Placed in sequence with the shots that logically would go before and after it in the story line, it becomes part of a storyboard.

The number of camera angles is virtually unlimited, and camera angles can be used to create unique presentation of the scene, such as the overhead shot in Figure 4-20. It shows the action as if the camera were positioned on top of the scene looking down. This extremely high angle (attic view) later would be used by Hitchcock in *Psycho*, when Norman stabs the inquisitive detective at the top of the stairs in the Victorian house.

## BUILDING THE STORYBOARD

At this point, you've become pretty adept at drawing the human figure in its simplest form. Let's start now to place them inside the individual rectangular frames that make up the shots.

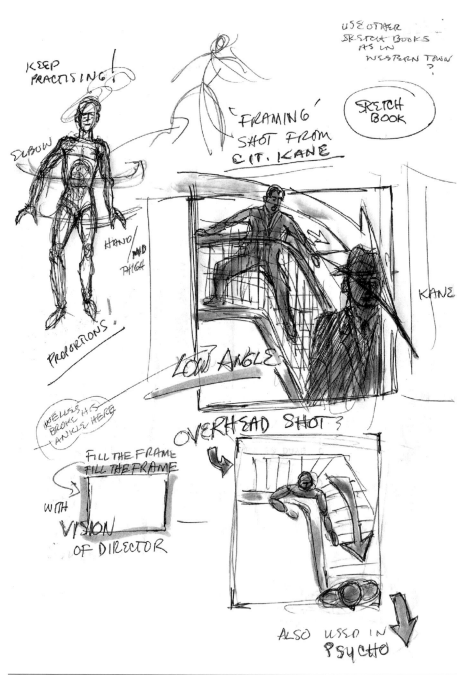

**Figure 4-20 Hart rough sketch of a shot from *Citizen Kane* plus the overhead shot, which was also used by Hitchcock in *Psycho*.**

To devise a good storyboard, ask yourself and your production heads the following questions:

- What is the story about?

- Who are the characters? And what is their motivation? (Motivation dictates blocking and framing, where the director places the actor within a given scene to convey the action of the script).

- What do they do and say, if dialogue is indicated?

- Which characters are in the foreground, middle ground, and background?

- Are they in conflict and with whom?

- Where does the conflict take place?

- When are long, medium and close-up shots necessary?

The answers to all these questions become clear when illustrated in the storyboard. Elements of period costumes should be fully researched. Attention must be paid to motivated light sources. Basic lighting of the main characters or lead actors in a film are lit through the use of the *key light* (strongest light on the face), *fill light* used to fill shadows (also called reflective light), and *back light* or hair light to separate the actor from the background. To quote the famous director Joseph von Sternberg (who directed the early Marlene Dietrich films) "Once you have mastered the key light, everything else falls into place." Lighting is covered in greater detail in Chapter 8.

KEY LIGHT, FILL LIGHT AND BACK LIGHT: Key light is the primary light shining directly on the focus of a scene, while fill light is used to reduce shadows and back light is light coming from behind the subject.

I did a storyboard for a screenplay by Lanny Foster, *Venus Mountain*. The screenplay contained some terrific action sequences that cried out for visualization. Figures 4-21 and 4-22 show a stick-figure interpretation for those of you who are still searching for a drawing style. Remember, I started out with this sequence by making very simple sketches in the margin of my copy of the script, as many directors do.

You follow the action that takes place between the characters Cardiff and Mary. As denoted in the script, Cardiff walks down the corridor, goes into his own large office, turns on the lights, and finally goes to his desk, all the while being stalked by a revengeful Mary, who eventually, gun in hand, confronts him in his office. This entire scene is observed by two assassins, one with binoculars and the other holding a gun, seen through one of the windows in the office building opposite.

Working with Mr. Foster (who also wanted to direct), we broke down the scene into the basic shots that it required with these initial rough sketches. He wanted to capture the intense flow of action that would build up to Mary threatening to kill Cardiff. So, keeping the continuity in mind, the power that well-designed frames and the use of fluid, not distracting camera work can bring to a scenario, I started with these thumbnail sketches. They follow the nine shots that we felt this particular page of the script needed to "tell the story" visually.

**Figure 4-21 *Venus Mountain* stick figure interpretation of the beginning of the script.**

Going from shots 1 through 11, you can follow the sequence of action:

Shot 1    A pan shot of Cardiff going down the corridor to open his door, filmed at a slightly lower angle, but not too low because he was seen from Mary's *point of view* (POV).

Shot 2    An OTS of Cardiff as he turns on the light in his dark office.

Shot 3    He throws his coat on the sofa, moves to the bar, to the window, to the desk and tape deck.

Shot 4    Cardiff in MGD, framed in the doorway of the office (Mary's POV) as her gun slowly intrudes into the left side of the frame.

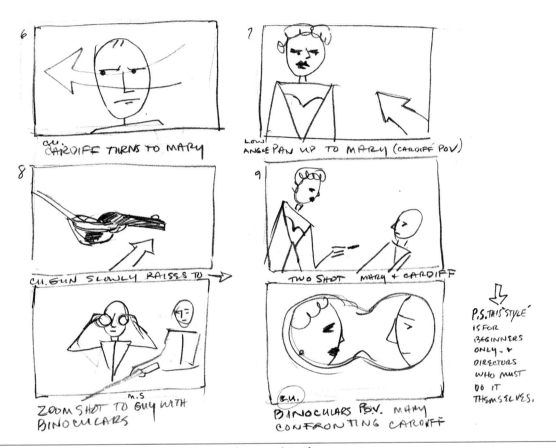

**Figure 4-22 *Venus Mountain* stick figure interpretation, continued.**

Shot 5    The barrel of the gun slowly advances from the left of the frame into the left center of the frame. (Keep the CU on the gun, with a wide angle lens as it moves toward Cardiff in MGD right of frame.) Cardiff looks up.

Shot 6    Cut to CU of Cardiff, where it freezes.

Shot 7    Low angle tilt-up to Mary (Cardiff POV).

Shot 8    Mary slowly raises the gun pointing at Cardiff.

Shot 9    Mary and Cardiff in a two-shot CU "facing off."

Shot 10    Cut to CU of assassin looking through binoculars at Mary and Cardiff.

Shot 11    CU of Mary and Cardiff framed in binoculars (assassin's POV).

This stick figure style is for beginners only or for directors who, like Spielberg, are not trained artists.

The next version (Figures 4-23 and 4-24) contains the same narrative and action sequence. I have fleshed out the figures and the locale with basic indications of light and shade and types of shots that the director and director of photography will need for the actual shooting.

## CLASSIC FILM EXAMPLES

Ridley Scott's Academy Award-winning film *Gladiator* (2005) tells the story of a Roman general who is betrayed and his family murdered by a corrupt prince (Figure 4-25). He comes to Rome as a gladiator to seek revenge. Although the film was of epic proportion, it also concentrated on the human element. The spectacular ancient Roman scenes were done with major help of VFX and CGI. In addition to his directing talent, Scott also did his own storyboards.

The famous still from *Gone with the Wind* shown in Figure 4-26 has several design elements going for it. Scarlett has just run in disgust from working in the hospital to find all of Atlanta trying to escape Sherman's advancing troops. Notice how production designer William Cameron Menzies and art director Lyle Wheeler designed the scene. Scarlett is taking off center stage on the platform, framed by the pillars on the left and a bird cage on the lower right of the wide angle frame. She is backlit, making her stand out from the moving mass behind her. The scene is framed by a series of buildings as the crowd pushes toward the action in the far background.

In Figure 4-27, I have broken up this dramatic scene into FGD, MGD and BGD. Three separate receding planes divide the scene and give it an in-depth, three-dimensional dynamic. Scarlet is in the FGD, the surging group behind her in the MGD and the distant train depot in the BGD. The backlighting from a bright sky, the wind and movement swirling the red dust and perfect movie scoring from Max Steiner all contribute to this memorable moment.

*The Beast from 20,000 Fathoms* (see Figure 4-28) was constructed using a technique called *claymation*. This was done with stop-motion 3D modeling to capture the movements of the dinosaur in this feature from 1953. The arrow obviously indicates his forward motion through the city. Notice that he is framed to the right center of the picture with his head turning inward to the action. The cars in the immediate FGD in this low angle shot not only are placed there for him to destroy but also to act as a framing device. The Godzilla image was updated by Spielberg in the *Jurassic Park* series and in *The Host,* a South Korean film by director Bong Joon-Ho released in the United States in 2007.

The sketch of *The Adventures of Baron Munchausen* (1989) directed by Terry Gilliam illustrates the design concept of the circle within the rectangle and clearly shows the

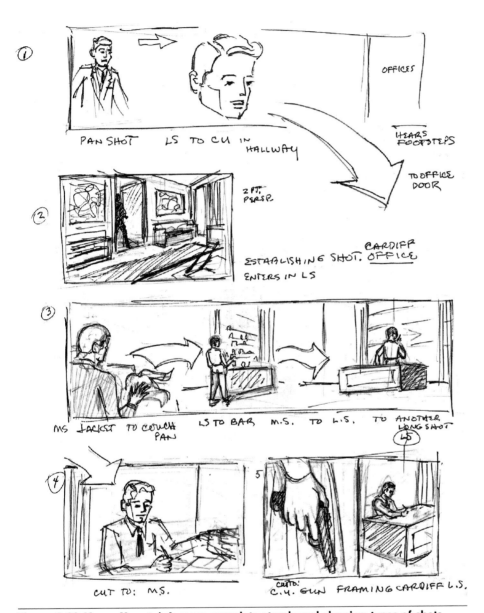

**Figure 4-23** *Venus Mountain's* more complete storyboard showing types of shots.

**Figure 4-24 Venus Mountain's more complete storyboard, continued.**

**Figure 4-25 The strong overhead sun with its resulting black shadows adds to the sense of defeat and the isolation of the gladiator. Note the contrast of the circle (shield) within the rectangular frame.**

line of action (Figure 4-29). It was shot against a greenscreen for a matte composite. They shot the actor first as a mask against the screen and then the background (sky) was added later, resulting in a dynamically visual shot aided by SFX.

Figures 4-30 and 4-31 illustrate a sequence of shots taken from *Terminator 2*, where the boy is pleading with the Terminator not to destroy himself. These storyboard sketches have been done in a very rough conceptual way using only a fine ballpoint pen. This touching scene has been broken down into the shots that the director felt told that part of the story. In other words, using just minimal lines, the concept of the scene (and each shot that makes it up) can be rendered with visual impact. There is ample imaging in this section of the storyboard that will easily serve as a guide not only for the director but also for the director of photography.

**Figure 4-26 Sketch of a scene from the classic Gone with the Wind, where Scarlett encounters the exodus from Atlanta.**

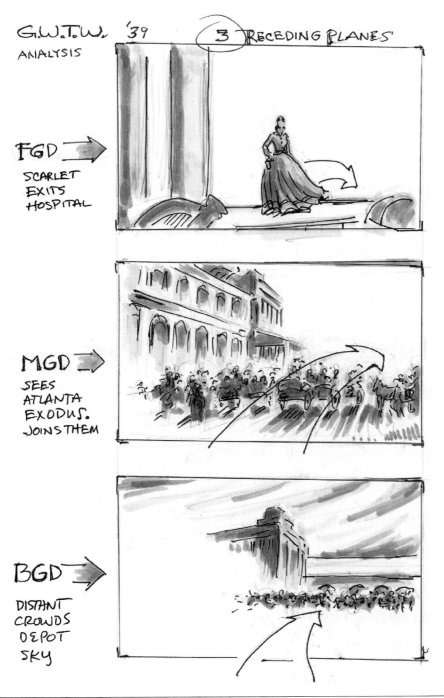

**Figure 4-27 Scene from _Gone with the Wind_ with the design elements broken into separate planes.**

**Figure 4-28 Sketch of *The Beast from 20,000 Fathoms*.**

**Figure 4-29 Sketch of an action scene from *The Adventures of Baron Munchausen*.**

**Figure 4-30 Storyboard from *Terminator 2 Judgment Day* showing violent action and traditional camera angles.**

**Figure 4-31 Continuation of a storyboard from *Terminator 2.***

## Tutorials

1. Watch movies in the American Film Institute's Top 100 films and examine the scene compositions for use of rule of thirds and visual planes.

2. Select a key scene from the screenplays for *Night at the Museum, Pan's Labyrinth, Dances with Wolves, Brokeback Mountain* and *Crash,* and storyboard each.

   Like the *Terminator 2* storyboard, format your frames with the horizontal rectangular film ratio of the wide screen. Be sure to pick the scene that has dramatic impact.

   Each storyboard should have at least 10 to 15 frames in it. For clarity, keep the drawings as simple as possible and always keeping in mind the visual needs of the preproduction team.

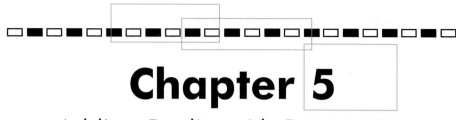

# Chapter 5
## Adding Reality with Perspective

Since the very invention of the cinema as a popular entertainment device in the late 19th century, it has been the aim of producers, directors, production designers, and directors of photography to reproduce and project our perceived three-dimensional reality onto a two-dimensional movie screen. Besides resorting to those 3D glasses, the filmmaker uses such filmic techniques as breaking up the photographed scene, or frame, into three specific planes discussed in Chapter 3: foreground (FGD), middle ground (MGD), and background (BGD). Adding interesting shot angles and vividly rendered light and shade to the filmed objects also enhances the three-dimensionality (Figure 5-1).

Techniques such as foreground framing literally "frame" the scene and also throw the viewers eye further into the mise-en-scene from FGD to MGD to BGD. Framing the shot helps focus attention to the primary action in the scene, the "off-center" center of interest. Paying attention to the geometric elements in any given shot by applying the use of ovals as a design factor also helps hold the attention of the audience.

### PERSPECTIVE

Most important however, is the application of the laws of perspective that augment and capture the three-dimensionality of the shot. Webster's Dictionary describes perspective as "the art of drawing objects on a plane surface to give impression of the relative distance of objects, indicated by the convergence of their receding lines." I like to think of perspective as to perceive, to view, to know, and to get a concept of 3D spaces.

Most images have at least one *vanishing point* (VP) – the point at which the receding lines in the image appear to meet. Except when viewing a flat plane placed horizontally in front of the viewer. Figure 5-2 taken at the Bodies Exhibit at the South Street Seaport in New York City is a vivid example – the exhibit signs and shape of the street stretch from FGD into the MGD, "meeting" in the upper right of the photo, just between the double doors in the brick building in the BGD. When an image has one vanishing point, because the viewer is looking straight at it, it is considered *one-point perspective*. The close-up in Figure 5-3 also showcases the anatomy of the human body.

VANISHING POINT: One or two points on the horizon line to which all converging lines will recede.

PERSPECTIVE: The art of representing on a two-dimensional plane what the viewer perceives as having three dimensions.

**Figure 5-1 This location shot illustrates high angle. Late afternoon sunlight causes strong vertical shadows. The highlighted umbrella carried by the "living statue" on the left of frame adds a vivid 3D aspect to its circular form.**

**Figure 5-2 This Hart photo of the Bodies Exhibit illustrates one point perspective aspect and vanishing point.**

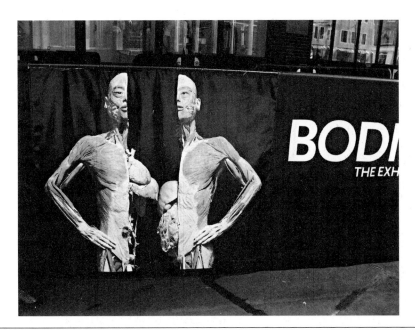

**Figure 5-3 Advertisement from the Bodies Exhibit shows the muscle structure of the human body in detail.**

The concept of receding planes is important because of all that takes place within its preconceived boundaries. Figure 5-4 illustrates each of the three divisions of space within its own picture plane or receding plane. The FGD (frontal plane) contains the chairs left of frame and two characters entering frame on the right. In the MGD are the units on wheels in front of the Fulton Market building on the left with the blue awning and the girl walking on the left. And the BGD occupies the area in the third, receding plane — the red brick buildings.

The two figures in the foreground and the girl walking on the left on the sidewalk are all walking toward the vanishing point. Can you find the vanishing point?

Who do we thank for this knowledge of receding planes and the use of perspective? Filippo Brunelleschi, architect and sculptor, the same genius who gave Florence his magnificent dome topping The Duomo in 1431. The shot of The Duomo (Figure 5-5) was taken from the street at an extremely low angle and exhibits several VPs.

The main focus is on the ribs framing the dome and the distant vanishing point they indicate. If you extended the verticals in the base supporting the dome, you would find a vanishing point approximately eight inches above the page. There are two vanishing points at the base of the support dome that eventually would meet the horizon line close to the bottom of the photo.

Brunelleschi's formulations of the laws of perspective were amplified by another genius of the Renaissance, the architect and writer, Leon Baptista Alberti who designed the famous façade of Santa Maria Novella in Florence.

**Figure 5-4 This Hart photo illustrates the concept the three receding planes.**

Wherever your eyes look, there is a built-in eye level – an imaginary horizon line that extends across your two pupils. If that line were extended to infinity, it would become a duplicate horizon line parallel to your eye level. On that horizon line or eye level, there will automatically be a VP directly in front of you (Figure 5-6). This vanishing point creates one-point perspective.

In addition, there are VPs at the far ends of your eye level, at 180° on either side of the one-point perspective VP (Figure 5-7). The far end occurs when you extend both your arms to your side until you can barely see them. These two VPs create two-point perspective.

ORTHOGONALS: The lines that lead to the vanishing point(s) in an image.

The perspective lines that lead to VPs are called *orthogonals*. In Figure 5-8 of FDR Drive in New York City, the VP is shown with the orthogonals receding off to the left of the page.

**Figure 5-5 Hart photo of The Duomo taken at an extremely low angle to show several vanishing points.**

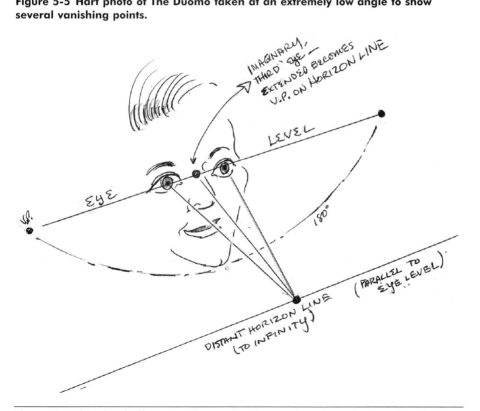

**Figure 5-6 This sketch illustrates the eye level as an imaginary horizon line that is always parallel to the distant horizon line.**

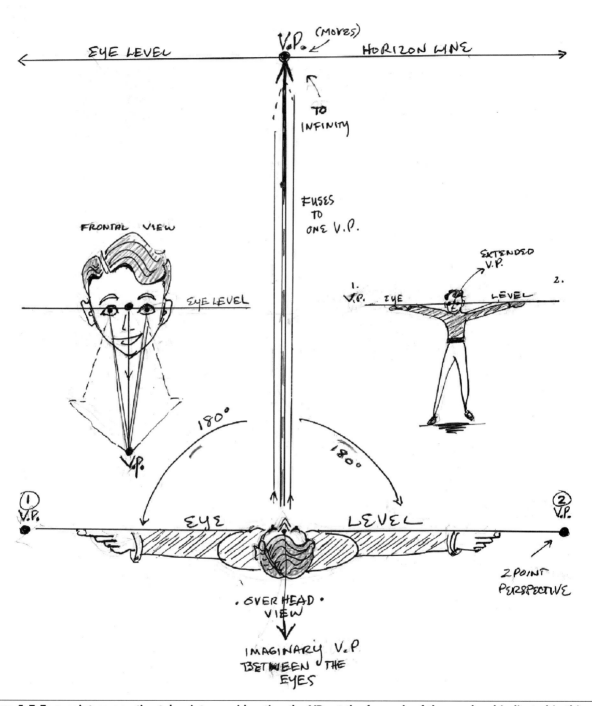

**Figure 5-7 Two-point perspective takes into consideration the VPs at the far ends of the eye level indicated in this drawing. Note in this sketch my indication of the imaginary vanishing point placed between the eyes from an overhead view.**

PROW:
A FRAMING
DEVICE

EYE LEVEL

ORTHOGONALS

V.P.

1 PT. PERSPECTIVE

**Figure 5-8 Orthogonals are lines that recede to the vanishing point.**

Figure 5-9 is an extreme low angle shot of the façade of a landmark building in New York City. As with the Duomo in Figure 5-5, the orthogonals go up and off the page to the VP. Look at the interpretive drawing (Figure 5-10) which illustrates these orthogonals.

Figure 5-11 shows one- and two-point perspective. I think that two-point perspective is only an issue when you are drawing the corner or corners of rooms, buildings, or objects like boxes.

A major point that must be acknowledged and understood is that the vanishing point is not stationary. It moves when we move, to reflect the way we are looking at a scene (Figure 5-12). I call this principle the *elevator effect*. Notice that when our figure moves from the first to the second or third floor that his horizon line and his vanishing point move vertically with him. Also, if our figure moves left to right his vanishing point continues to move with him on his horizon line.

ELEVATOR EFFECT: Our eye level, horizon line and VPs move as we do.

**Figure 5-9 Extreme low angle building shot that duplicates the same perspective as The Duomo photo (Figure 5-5).**

When we look at Figure 5-13, we see the vanishing point looking straight down from a high angle, such as an aerial shot or bird's-eye view.

There is no question that perspective can be intimidating to the beginning artist. But, as with all storyboarding skills, examinations of others' work and practice will help develop and improve these skills.

The cowboy sketch in Figure 5-14 is a good example of the dramatic use of perspective in FGD, MGD and BGD; VPs; and use of light and shade; with the character placed off center to the left of frame. Every classic cowboy film has the hero in a face-off with the villain on Main Street. In this shot, the saloon is in the left FGD and the general store on the right is in the MGD. The grain store on the left is also in the MGD and appears half the normal size. The church on the right in the BGD appears normal height.

The director has the perspective of the shot in mind and that will dictate the camera placement and angle. This will be storyboarded for the director to see before shooting it, in collaborating with the director of photography, art director or set designer. Using a low camera angle, the actor will appear taller and more imposing. Even the street itself will look more menacing if shot below eye level.

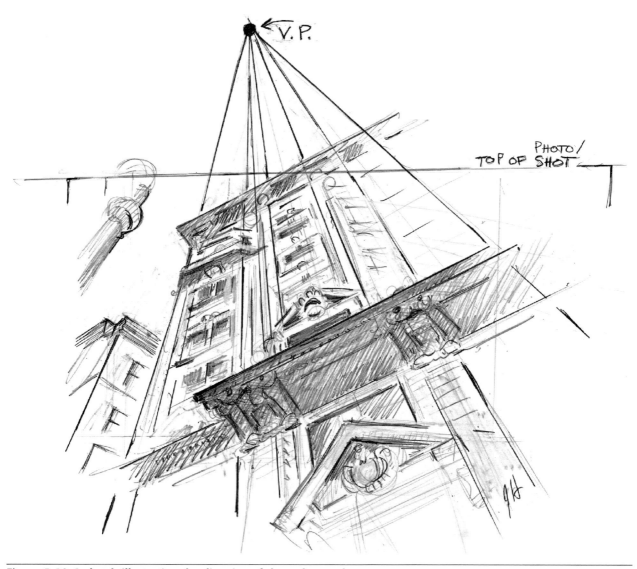

**Figure 5-10 A sketch illustrating the direction of the orthogonals.**

Note that all the lines of the building go back to one VP, indicated by the dot just to the left of the church. This scene also makes use of *forced perspective*, where objects in the BGD are created disproportionately smaller than the objects in the FGD. This makes the actor and buildings in the FGD appear much larger and the BGD appear much farther away.

FORCED PERSPECTIVE: Making the FGD objects seem larger and BGD objects seem smaller by creating them out of proportion to one another. This creates a greater distance in the shot.

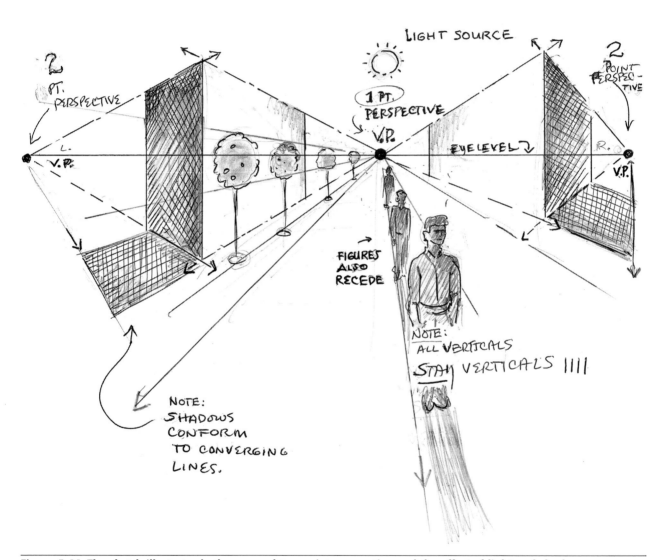

**Figure 5-11 The sketch illustrates both one- and two-point perspective and the effect of light and shade.**

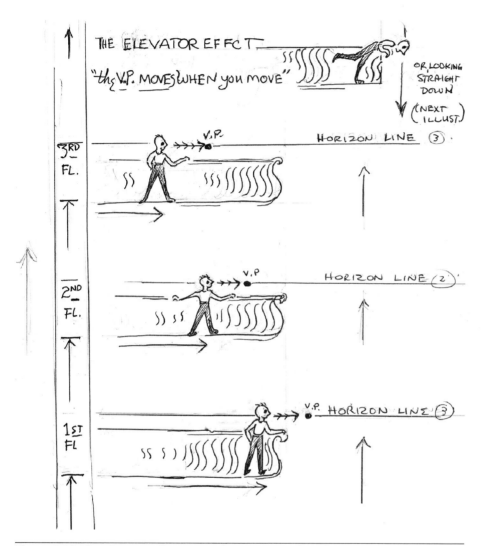

**Figure 5-12 The elevator effect states that no matter how far you move vertically or horizontally, your eye level and vanishing point stay with you.**

Figure 5-15 is a storyboard that uses the technique of vanishing points, indications of motion, light and shade and close-up. The character is centered in the frame of a low angle shot in the hall. Light and shadows come from the windows on the right of the frame. In the next frame, she is placed to the right of the frame and an arrow indicates her movement through the doorframe on the left. She is looking into the interior of the classroom filled with light and shade from the windows on the right. It is one-point perspective because the angle of the shot is taken from her POV

★ THE ELEVATOR EFFECT, ②

★
"THE V.P. MOVES WHEN you MOVE",
WHILE ALWAYS STAYING ON THE
EYE LEVEL / HORIZON LINE,
WHETHER MOVING VERTICALLY
OR HORIZONTALLY ★

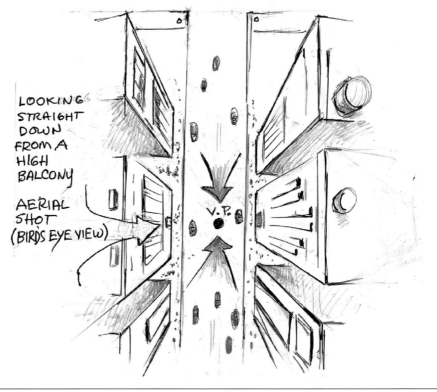

LOOKING
STRAIGHT
DOWN
FROM A
HIGH
BALCONY

AERIAL
SHOT
(BIRD'S EYE VIEW)

V.P.

**Figure 5-13 Sketch of an aerial view of the elevator effect, as if we are looking straight down from a balcony.**

**Figure 5-14 Sample production sketch showing VP, perspective and light sources.**

standing in the front of the classroom looking to the back of the room. And the last frame is an extreme close-up of her, off center to the left of the frame.

A practiced, trained eye in three-dimensional composition will aid the storyboard artist to meet any and all preproduction needs. With the emphasis I have given to the principles of design, perspective, light and shade, the storyboard artist will be able to make on-the-spot rough or concepts sketches of key scenes in the script when asked by the director to satisfy his pre-viz requirements.

## CLASSIC FILM EXAMPLES

When I look at a painting, photograph or motion picture the first thing I ask is "Does it project exceptional composition or design? Classic films, many of which are used as examples in this book, and were inspired by Renaissance painters and their interpretation of reality in their oeuvré and influence the work of such great directors of photography as Gregg Toland, Carl Freund and Gordon Parks. The masterful work of production designers such as Ken Adam and Martin Scorsese's favorite designer, Dante Ferretti, have also been influenced by art history. As one famous

**Figure 5-15 This storyboard by Ulrich Zeidler, 1999, www.ulrichzeidler.com, www.storyboards.nl shows various aspects of motion, light and close-ups.**

art historian said "Life is short, art is long." All of the above artists are in the forefront of superlative film great design.

In Figure 5-16 from the premiere detective story *The Maltese Falcon* (1941), Humphrey Bogart as Sam Spade looks down the embankment at his murdered partner's body. It is an example not only of a dramatic low angle shot, but also the use of two-point perspective and two light sources. Imagine a line running straight across the top of the FGD rocks (this is your eye level line). Out of our sight lines are two vanishing points, one to the right of the frame and one to the left. All the lines that make up the fence in the FGD and the flat walls facing us (receding planes) will converge to the VP at eye level or the horizon line to the left of the frame. The angled wall directly behind Sam is made up of lines that converge back to their own VP just below the streetlight. All in all this is an excellently designed scene by director John Huston.

Figure 5-17 is a concept sketch for a poster idea – a montage of the *Batman* movie series illustrating the use of a low angle shot where the compression of space gives visual drama and the forced perspective gives added depth and movement to the sketch.

I redesigned the Fox logo for the 21$^{st}$ century in two-point perspective (Figure 5-18). I have made the horizon line quite clear and indicated where both the right and left VPs are located.

**Figure 5-16 Interpretative sketch of a scene from *The Maltese Falcon* showing one- and two-point perspective, low angle and several different light sources.**

FORCED PERSPECTIVE!

**Figure 5-17 Montage for the *Batman* series.**

**Figure 5-18 Concept sketch for a new Fox logo.**

*Vertigo*, directed by Alfred Hitchcock in 1958, includes the shot in Figure 5-19 of actor, James Stewart, the lead character who suffers from severe vertigo. In this scene, he's going down the tower steps. The seriously distorted one-point perspective plus the addition the special effect of having the structure sway adds to the terror the audience experiences with the character.

The shot in Figure 5-20 is from *Red River* (1948), a Howard Hawks western. An illustration of *atmospheric perspective*, referred to as the law of content, occurs when the scene does not consist of linear perspective but rather is constructed of foreground framing, middle ground actions and backgrounds that are out of focus to give added depth. This shot shows that atmospheric perspective can consist simply of a view of cattle in the MGD plane along with the cowboys who drive them to market. The shot is beautifully framed in the FGD with the trees. The arrow indicates the line of action. When you place a shot in any film, there has to be a unity of space, a unity of composition and a pre-viz placement of people and objects.

HITCHCOCK                    VERTIGO '58

1 PT. PERSPECTIVE

V.P. ?

**Figure 5-19 In this scene from *Vertigo*, the sketch illustrates extreme high angle one-point perspective.**

At FRAMING OF DYNAMIC MOVEMENT
RECESSION OF SPACE –

RED RIVER

**Figure 5-20 A scene from *Red River* showing the framing of dynamic movement and use of contrasting light and shade as well as backlighting.**

The frame (the four sides that contain the selected subject matter) is the picture's boundary of reality. Remember that we, as artists, select from the millions of images that exist around us and then pinpoint, emphasize and rearrange a selected few of these images for use in the storyboard. One of the basic composition faux pas that I often see occurs when the artist is not aware of or ignores that basic design element, the principle of thirds. Simply stated, the image behind the frontal plane should be divided into thirds (already discussed in Chapter 3).

Any sequence of shots or frames chosen from the script should contain images that will illustrate all the visual talents of the director, director of photography, production designer and the storyboard artist – that's called collaboration.

Great design is about developing a sense of proportion. In Figure 5-21, a sketch of a set shot from *Casino Royale* (2006), we see James Bond waiting for the "action" call. The camera is at an extreme low angle, the director is explaining what comes next, and the film crew is ready to follow the actor's movements. Even this behind-the-scenes shot demonstrates good composition and design because the central figure is off-center. A series of ovals frame the shot – notice the boom mic and the frame of the reflector. The guy holding the boom mic, the director, and focus puller all frame and indicate the center of interest, James Bond.

**Figure 5-21 Set shot from *Casino Royale*.**

Hopefully you are convinced at this point that the laws of perspective and design should govern your personal view of reality. Once these rules are mastered and implemented in your storyboard, drawn by hand or CGI, your can consider yourself a professional.

**Tutorials**

1. Buy, or rent or go to see at least six recent films. Take a medium-sized sketch pad with you. As you watch the film, make quick sketches of scenes you feel are particularly stunning or graphically interesting. Draw your sketches simply, focusing on basically observed geometric patterns of the scene before you. Make dozens of sketches as you watch.

2. Go over the sketches when you get home. Ask yourself these questions:

   a. Did I capture an interesting use of perspective?

   b. Is there any use of forced or atmospheric perspective?

   c. Did the production designer follow the rule of thirds?

   d. Were the shots framed in a visually interesting way?

   e. Was the rule of off-center obeyed?

   f. Was there use of varied and interesting angles?

   g. Did the light plots enhance the light and shade of the actors and their environment?

   h. What design elements enhanced the three-dimensionality of the scenes or shots?

   i. What was the overall "look" of the film, and did it work?

3. Always keep your sketches and notes for future reference. Make up a portfolio for your own use and never throw anything away.

# Chapter 6
## Design, Composition and Color

Great film design is about developing a sense of proportion, a feeling for what "works." What "reads" well beyond the frame or frontal plane? Large trees framing the cattle run in *Red River*? Small trees? No trees at all? The artist's entire effort should be to capture the viewers' attention and keep them visually stimulated. Viewers want to see the results of your creative eye. An awareness of the various planes that exist behind the picture plane will help you think not only in terms of great composition but also three-dimensionally. Producing a film requires intensive collaborative efforts. The storyboard artist, working from the concepts given by the director, can be one of the key creative figures helping to integrate all of the diverse elements that go into developing the "look" of the finished product. When dealing with design and color, basic design elements come first and then you add color for visual impact.

### DRAWING HUMANS IN ACTION

Go to the How-To section of any bookstore and you will find many "how to draw" books written specifically to train burgeoning artists. Books with particular emphasis on drawing the human figure in action will be of immense help for the beginning storyboard artist (see Figure 6-1). For those who will be taking film courses, classes leaning specifically toward the unique art form we know as storyboarding will be taught and mastered.

Try using stick figures, cylinders or scribbled figures to make the rough sketches of motion. It might be difficult at first, but it's a start and you will become more proficient with more practice (Figure 6-2).

As an additional aid in delineating the human figure, I suggest you purchase an anatomical model, usually made of wood with pliable arms, legs, torso and head like the one in Figure 6-3. The inexpensive models stand about nine inches tall and are great for rendering the proportions of the body for your storyboard images.

When I was a graduate art student taking a sculpture class, the concept of light falling on three-dimensional forms became even more obvious. I learned how light and shade shape an object or figure giving it its solid form, weight and placement in reality (Figure 6-4).

**Figure 6-1 A figure running, from stick figure to full dimension, delineated with light and shade.**

Don't just sketch the model from straight on. Set the arms, legs, hands, and head in a running position. Then close your left eye and, pretending your right eye is the camera lens, pick up the figure or model and "zoom in" on it from different angles – low angles, high angles, even turn it slowly in front of your "lens." Sketch the model from these diverse positions. This technique will help you develop a more creative eye for your storyboards. Unusual angles make for more interesting storyboards while you are also improving your drawing skills (Figure 6-5).

## Human Proportions

- Figures 6-6 and 6-7 show the universally accepted basic proportions used by art students for drawing references. They are: The size of the human head is referred to as the *head length*, from chin to the top of the head.

- The height of one's hand is equal to the size of one's face.

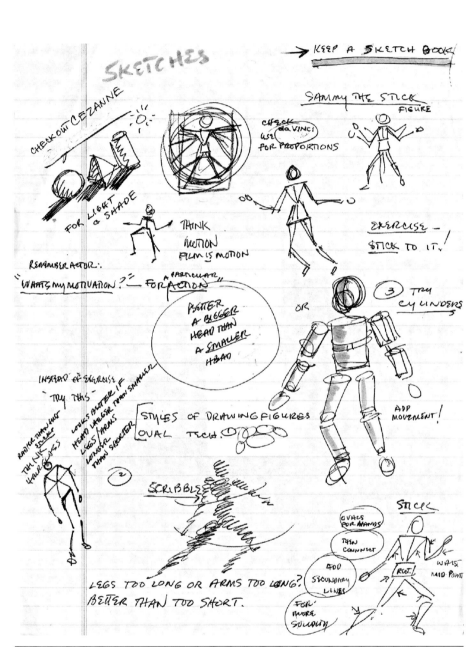

**Figure 6-2 Sketchbook exercises eventually lead to mastery.**

**Figure 6-3 Use an anatomical model for figure movement.**

- The human head, as in all of our golden mean proportions is divided into thirds:
  - ⅓ from the chin to the base of the nose
  - ⅓ from the base of the nose to the eyebrows (or ears)
  - ⅓ from the eyebrows to the top of the head
- The average male's body height is 7½ heads tall; the same would apply to the female body, which is usually shorter.

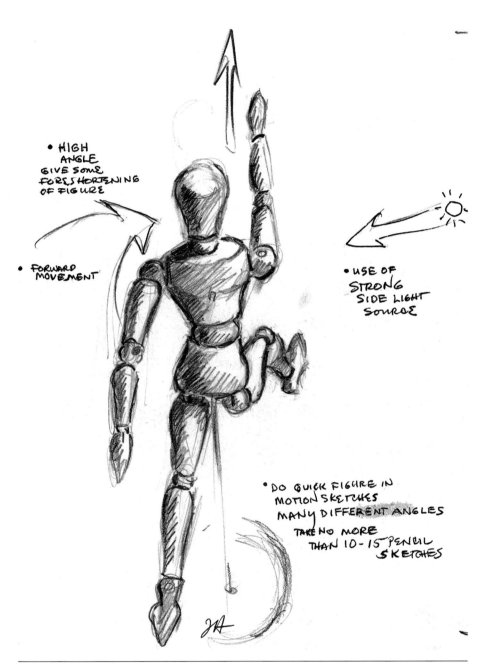

**Figure 6-4 Include light and shade in drawing of the model.**

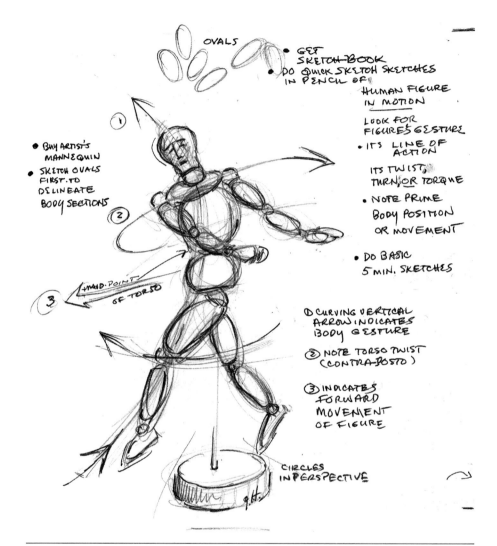

**Figure 6-5 Use the model to sketch the human figure in action.**

- The halfway point from head to toe would be at the pubic arch.

- The length of the arm to the elbow coincides with the mid-point of the torso or trunk.

- The tip of the hand held straight down against the thigh approximates half the body height.

- The width from shoulder to shoulder is normally two head lengths. Female shoulders are narrower.

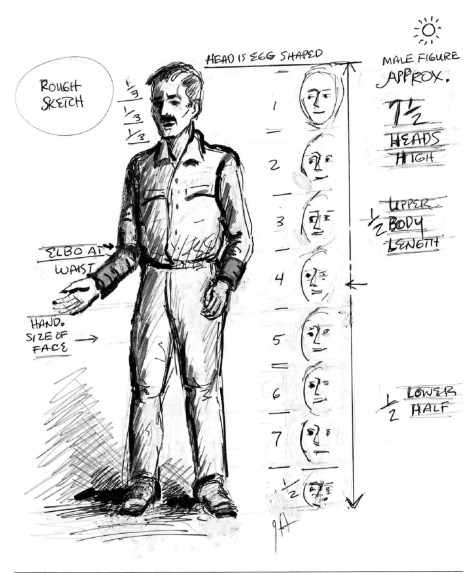

ROUGH SKETCH

HEAD IS EGG SHAPED

$\frac{1}{3}$
$\frac{1}{3}$
$\frac{1}{3}$

ELBO AT WAIST

HAND. SIZE OF FACE →

1
2
3
4
5
6
7
$\frac{1}{2}$

MALE FIGURE APPROX.

$7\frac{1}{2}$ HEADS HIGH

$\frac{1}{2}$ UPPER BODY LENGTH

$\frac{1}{2}$ LOWER HALF

**Figure 6-6 Proportion for drawing the human body.**

- The female pelvic area is wider and legs of the female form are normally longer than those of the male figure.

See also the gesture illustrations and other references to anatomy.

I have indicated in Figure 6-7 of the human head what I call the *Picasso line*. In his Cubism phase, Picasso loved to break up the human head into two or three sections or more. My Picasso line divides the head into only two sections. This line follows

**PICASSO LINE:** To illustrate the sculptural form of a face it is a line that follows the contours of the face from forehead to neck – resulting also in a "profile" of its own.

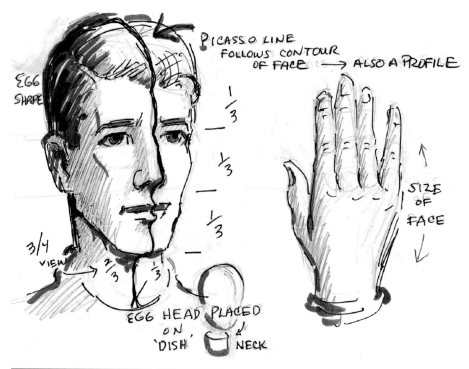

**Figure 6-7 The Picasso line.**

the contours of the face from the forehead to the chin — aiding us to sense this sculptural quality of the human head and giving the indication of a full profile.

## LIGHT AND SHADOW

I would like to illustrate some very basic drawing methods that will aid you in developing, I hope, your own special style as a storyboard artist. For me, being aware of the three dimensionality that exists in the perceived world around us is of primary importance because it will motivate any drawing, even the simplest one (Figure 6-8).

Where there is a light source, the object that its rays fall upon will cast a shadow. You can actually draw figures just by indicating the play of light and shade falling on and shaping them (see Figure 6-9). This light and shade depiction on a figure or object will give that object its three-dimensionality.

I remember, in a college art class, the drawing instructor insisting that I draw the light and shade on a hat over and over again until I rendered its structure correctly. The light falling from a side window caused the side of the hat opposite the light to

**Figure 6-8 A simple sketch of the human figure.**

**Figure 6-9 A sketch from *Apocalypse Now* (1979); notice the reflected light on the fuselage.**

**Figure 6-10 Interpretive sketch from *Pirates of the Caribbean*.**

fall into shadow. That shadow must conform to and shape the structure of the hat, thus giving it its three-dimensionality. Observe the light and shade of the hat, face and hands of Johnny Depp from *Pirates of the Caribbean* depicted in Figure 6-10.

## THE IMPORTANCE OF COLOR

Let's take a moment now to discuss the importance of color, the psychology of color, its tones, hues and intensities and their various uses in films. Just check out GamFusion filters (www.gamonline.com), a complete line of color filters and diffusion material for film lighting or gel sheets of different colors used to change the mood of a scene. They have swatch books and you can see how many shades of the color spectrum are available to the cinematographer.

**Figure 6-11** *Amarcord* (1974) illustrates a "light" comedy.

To change the tone or mood of a given scene, two points are to be kept in mind: comedy is light (see Figure 6-11) and tragedy is dark. We might say that melodrama can be a combination of both. That does not mean that the movie has to be shot completely in tones of gray.

It is not difficult to consider that "light" colors are happy. Yellow denotes cheerful, optimistic, summertime and so on. Blue, outside of being a background for puffy white clouds is often used to denote a depressing scene or night shot. Note in the sketch from *Batman & Robin* (1997) in Figure 6-12, that blue is the dominant color of Mr. Freeze. Also note the arrows that indicate the action lines or movement of the body and the use of ovals and cylinders in the drawing.

The primary colors red, yellow and blue can be mixed into secondary colors. Yellow and blue make green, red and yellow are orange, and so forth. Purple (blue and red), especially when a bit of black is added, starts to lean into the darker spectrums. Red reads danger and all you have to do is watch its extensive use in films as a visual jolt for murder and mayhem. Just remember, save red for something really "hot."

**Figure 6-12 An analytical sketch indicating the use of arrows for action direction for Mr. Freeze from *Batman & Robin*.**

- NOTE USE OF OVALS    • COMPOSITION / FIGURE    • 3D SPACE  RECEDING DISTANCE
- FIGURE TURN                         OFF·CENTER.    GREEN TONES WITH TOUCH OF RED.

**Figure 6-13 *The Quiet Man* (1952) illustrates the soothing effect of nature and the color green; the environment also emphasizes the contrast with O'Hara.**

Green is the color that projects calm and the environs of the forest, like John Wayne walking at ease through the lush Irish landscapes in John Ford's *The Quiet Man* (1952), until he encounters Maureen O'Hara, with her flaming red hair (Figure 6-13).

As with mixing shades of black and white to blend gray tones, color can also be "grayed down" or toned down to soften its effect. As with any art form, save the blatant, strongest color for the strongest image, the peak moments in the script. Reds especially should be used very carefully.

In other words, don't give it all away at once. Too much of anything can be boring. Learn early to be subtle and save the fireworks for the Fourth of July, or as background high jinks for a climatic kiss between Cary Grant and Grace Kelly in Alfred Hitchcock's *To Catch a Thief* (1955). Watch this film and ask yourself if it would work as well in black and white? Is the production design strong enough to hold up on its own without color?

For the superb use of Technicolor, screen the 1940 *The Thief of Baghdad* (shown frequently on TMC)—it won an Oscar for cinematography. Watch for the shot when the evil Jaffar, in a contrasting black costume) persuades the princess to smell a lustrous blue rose so she will fall into a spell. In close-up, the razor sharp shot of the blue rose has maximum visual impact.

According to French Impressionist painter Pierre-Auguste Renoir, "The best color use can be observed right there in nature and you will note, nature uses its chromatic repertoire with a great deal of discretion." Check out the use of color by the Impressionists in any art history book.

Techniques like putting a dash of red off-center in a green landscape or a splash of orange in a predominantly gray scene always give the shot a visual punch. The color orange in its various shades and hues can also be used advantageously especially when it's tinged with red. It is a natural for sunsets and for the extremely high incident of explosions in current blockbusters.

Similar to the tones in a black-and-white film, one can use monochromatic colors, which are colors, shades and color hues based on one tertiary color like a burnt umber (the right mix of orange and purple). A classic example of the subtle use of color with soft, yet luminous intensities is the Japanese masterpiece *Gate of Hell* (1953), which received Oscars for best foreign film and costume design. The sundrenched colors Van Gogh used in all his paintings are brilliantly captured in *Lust for Life*, Vincente Minnelli's Oscar winning 1956 film. The film, shot in and around Arles in the South of France, was nominated for Best Art Direction, Set Decoration and Color (Figure 6-14).

**Figure 6-14 A sketch of Kirk Douglas portraying Van Gogh in a posed publicity shot for *Lust for Life*.**

## Black and White

Filming in black and white is making a come back. It was used to great effect in Steven Spielberg's *Schindler's List* (1993) and more recently in *Good Night and Good Luck* (2005) and *Sin City* (2005) though the film was actually released on color stock, giving it a richer chiaroscuro effect. This popular film style, derived from the legendary detective movies like *The Maltese Falcon*, has been tagged *film noir*, which I translate as "Shoot it inexpensively at night, in and out of the black shadows."

The common theory behind film noir is that expensive sets and lighting equipment were scarce during World War II. The films were shot in low light, making audiences less likely to notice the lack of elaborate sets and the wartime cutback on the use of electricity. We can see the influence of the film noir genre in Jean-Luc Godard's *Breathless* (1960) and in the searing drama *The 400 Blows* (1959), Figure 6-15, by the stimulating Francois Truffaut.

Truffaut also gave us *Day for Night* (1973), his Oscar winning "how to make a movie" script conceit. *Day for Night* could have had just as much dramatic impact

**FILM NOIR:** French term for dark cinema. Popular black-and-white films mainly from the 40s and 50s. Used chiaroscuro high contrast light and shade.

400 BLOWS '59
TRUFFAUT

FIGURE (OVALS) OFF CENTER FRAMING

**Figure 6-15 In this Hart sketch from film noir classic *The 400 Blows*, note the figure done in ovals and framed off-center.**

PSYCHO

OFF CENTER | STRONG LIGHT + SHADE

**Figure 6-16 Scene from *Psycho* is off-center with strong light and shade.**

if it had been shot in black and white. Truffaut was tremendously influenced by Alfred Hitchcock's *Psycho* (1960), shown in Figure 6-16. Who needed color in the infamous shower scene? Hitchcock decided that the most realistic looking blood could be simulated best in black and white with chocolate syrup. Another example of Truffaut's homage to Hitchcock is evident in his "dark" comedy, *The Bride Wore Black,* released in 1968.

Although most current films are in color, the storyboard artist can save money for the producers and give them the visceral impact they seek with storyboards executed in black and white with the added dimension of gray shadows.

**Figure 6-17 Our Western hero faces off with the bad guy.**

## DESIGN AND COMPOSITION

Good design always means understanding and interpreting the visual demands of the script. Figure 6-17 shows a shot from a generic western, where our action hero frames the scene to the left with CU of his gun in the extreme left FGD. An open gate occupies the MGD while the barn and his nemesis occupy the BGD.

In the sketch from *Tiko and the Shark* (1966) in Figure 6-18, the FGD is made up of two large vertical tree limbs on which fish are being dried. The MGD has the boy moving off-center left of the frame on a horizontal limb. In the BGD to the right of the frame, you see a girl with outstretched arms. Water receding toward the horizon could be considered a fourth plane. The figures have been rendered simply, but solidly.

RECEDING PLANES • PLACEMENT OF FIGURES
• FRGD FRAMING.                        OFF-CENTER
SOFT OVERHEAD LIGHTING

TIKO + THE SHARK

**Figure 6-18 This is a sketch from *Tiko and the Shark* (1966). Its misty gray overtones and original FGD framing add to the visual character.**

The circle as a design element is used in the scene from the film *2001* (1968) in Figure 6-19, which shows the 3D reality of objects and forms existing in a given space.

One of the most famous films of the 20th century is the silent film *Battleship Potemkin* (1925), directed by Sergei Eisenstein. Frames 76 through 84 (Figure 6-20) show us the design elements and conflict of forces at work in each dynamic shot. They have been drawn very simply but they still convey the sequence of action. In frame 85 (Figure 6-21), the mother is shot and starts to fall. It has been rendered in full dimensional light and shade. With practice, patience and persistence, you will soon be able to make the transition from simple figures to fully dimensional renderings.

2001

*John Hart*

**Figure 6-19 The 3D circle as a design element is evident in this shot from *2001*.**

If I were to recommend one book that is a compendium of the best of Hollywood's films, it is Ronald Haver's *David O. Selznick's Hollywood* (1987). It's full of high quality films from this prolific producer. Selznick reached his peak with the spectacular *Gone with the Wind* (1939, directed by Victor Fleming) and, in contrast, the rich black-and-white cinematography of *Rebecca* (1940, directed by Alfred Hitchcock). You will find at least 1,500 illustrations from preproduction conferences involving storyboarding, set design, costume design and set decoration, all the way up to the actual production scheduling involving many original shots and camera setups (see Figure 6-22). This volume alone gives you insight into the multiple areas of visual enhancement that make for breathtaking films.

SOLDIERS ENTER LEFT — EXIT SCREEN RIGHT

FRAME 76

SOLDIERS ENTER LEFT — EXIT RIGHT

79

FRAME 82

SOLDIERS 77

MOTHER WITH CHILD ADVANCES TO SOLDIERS

BODIES OF FALLEN

80

SHADOW OF SOLDIERS FALL ACROSS MOTHER + CHILD

83

"LISTEN TO ME DON'T SHOOT!"

78

"MY CHILD IS HURT!"

81

84

SOLDIERS FIRE

**Figure 6-20** *Battleship Potemkin* (1925) frames 76 to 84.

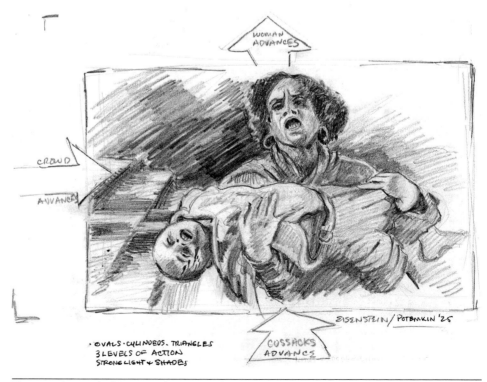

WOMAN ADVANCES

CROWD

ADVANCE

EISENSTEIN / POTEMKIN '25

COSSACKS ADVANCE

· OVALS · CYLINDERS · TRIANGLES
3 LEVELS OF ACTION
STRONG LIGHT + SHADES

**Figure 6-21** *Battleship Potemkin* (1925) frame 85.

**Figure 6-22 An interpretive sketch showing Menzies checking camera positions against his storyboard for *The Devil and Miss Jones* (1941).**

## Tutorials

1. Draw scenes of figures in action in black and white. You can use everyday scenes or interpret scenes from films.

2. Draw the same scene again using color. Check your composition and design and pay particular attention to light and shadows.

3. Being able to draw the human figure quickly and accurately requires a great deal of discipline on your part. Don't forget to carry that sketchbook with you and make sketches from everyday life.

# Chapter 7

## Illustrating Action in Your Storyboard

Creating well-drawn, motivated figures that kinetically move in an interesting way through the 3D space of the film is one of the primary jobs of the storyboard artist. A finished storyboard covering all the basic shots tells the story and is an invaluable aid to the entire preproduction team. Vivid images from a strong director and a storyboard illustrating their robust style complements the intensity of the action and the raw emotions of the characters. The shots from important films in this chapter demonstrate how the dynamic placement of figures within the continuity of the storyboard frames has to be rendered simply yet effectively. Indications of sets constructed or actual buildings and locations used must be illustrated in the storyboard artist's renderings, remembering that sets are background for the action.

The use of special effects, computer graphics (CG) and the compositing of different images enhance the continuing action of the storyline and the VFX must be indicated and illustrated in the storyboard.

*Superman Returns* (2006), directed by Bryan Singer, is a super sendoff of the previous versions and is considered by many to be the best. It has a strong backstory and an interesting new story line, with strong performances from all the leads, plus spectacular new VFX. Nominated for an Oscar for Best Achievement in Visual Effects, this film would make one agree with the ads for the film. Talk about action! Talk about adventure! Talk about superb visuals!

I went to see this new version of *Superman Returns* at a local IMAX equipped theatre, and the film was indeed awesome. The IMAX projection – with its humongous curved screen and high-definition projection – increased the feeling of a 3D world. Added to the visual thrill were several scenes that were shown in 3D – the coming new rage in Hollywood. *Superman Returns* is a terrific contemporary showcase for the very latest digital/CGI/greenscreen technology. For the showing, I took along my trusty 8 × 10 sketchpad and sketched many key scenes very quickly in the semi-darkness.

I have selected just five of my favorites for demonstration purposes only. I had to sketch fast, but have, frankly, gotten quite good at it with practice. Keeping in mind the geometric construction of any image helped make my drawing easier, as it will be with yours. I hand-drew the individual scenes denoting action. Arrows indicate direction of movement.

Frame 1. I tried to capture the iconic image of the new Superman (created by Scott Marsden). And although we know that he is suspended on wires against a greenscreen with multiple tech assistants pointing fans at him, the masterful use of the current CGI technology causes us to suspend our belief.

Frame 2. The teenage Superman tests his new flying skill, taking off from a handy water tower.

Frame 3. In this low-angle action shot, Clark Kent is in a major hurry to change into his Superman persona. The character action is slanted at an angle to his left to add to the feeling of swift movement from BGD to MGD to FGD.

Frame 4. Superman raises an entire subterranean city from the depths of the ocean. Very impressive shot, showing imaginative compositing of several elements, the model of the island city, the turbulent digital sky with added lighting, and the ocean with the huge opening left by the island topped by the figure of Superman lifting the whole shebang.

Frame 5. Another shot demonstrating fabulous CGI and the composting of various images. The packed ballpark, upper left of center, waiting to be destroyed by the plummeting airplane, entering dramatically into the upper right frame is stopped by the invincible super hero. This dynamic placement of the digitized components makes for a white-knuckle ending in this super sequence.

Getting the knack of drawing the human figure is not easy, but here are some more ideas that will help. Some of the drawings in Figure 7-3 are little more than doodles, but in drawing even these simple exercises, you will become more facile at rendering the human figure in motion. After dozens and dozens of attempts, eventually you will develop a style of your own, even if it is crude at first. Refer back to the development drawings of Chapter 6 and keep the wooden artist's model handy.

In these sketches, you can start out with a stick figure, but you don't have to stay with it. You can simply double the lines as seen in frame 2.

In frame 3, I added ovals for the body shapes, remembering the principle of threes — upper arm, lower arm and hand; upper leg, lower leg and foot; and the chest, the waist and the hip. Even the human head, as in frame 8, is divided into three sections: the top of the head to the eyebrows, the eyebrows to the base of the nose, and from the base of the nose to the chin. Notice that the ears always are placed in the middle third between the eyebrow and the nose.

In frame 4, I used a coil or spiral technique to flesh out the stick technique. In frame 5, I broke up the various thirds of the body parts into cylinders.

**Figure 7-1 Superman storyboard frames 1, 2 and 3.**

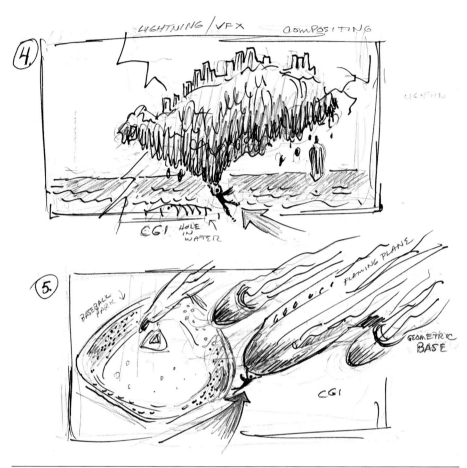

**Figure 7-2 Superman storyboard frames 4 and 5.**

Try each of these techniques and see which might work best for you. By frame 6, I hope you will have arrived at a possible style of your own, showing the figure drawn more completely, so that by frame 7 you can add some simple indication of light and shade. All you have to keep in mind is this: Where is the light source? For instance, if you place a bright light to the right of an egg (which has the same general shape as the human head), the left side will fall into shadow.

Keep in mind those all-important proportions and keep comparing the size of the head to the width of the shoulders, the bend of the elbow is at the waist, the elbow one-half the length of the arm.

Figure 7-4 is a sketch from *Reign over Me* (2007), where Adam Sandler's character lost his family in the 9/11 attack on New York City. He searches out his old friend

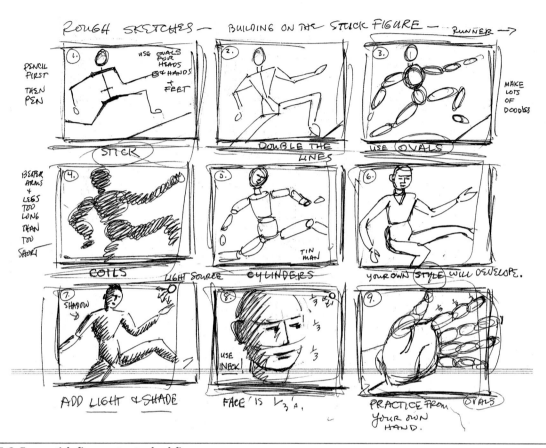

**Figure 7-3 From stick figures to stacked figures.**

and roommate, played by Don Cheadle, to help him deal with his grief. In the film, Sandler is searching through material that will help him make new life adjustments.

This interpretation sketch is an example of *implied action* or an action waiting to happen. The moment itself with Sandler holding the document is fraught with future implications as Cheadle gives moral support. It is a quiet but intense part of the narrative flow.

Figure 7-5 is a sketch from *A Hard Day's Night* (1967). This classic romp, exuberantly directed film by Richard Lester and starring the Fab Four, exudes all of the kinetic energy anyone could want in any film. The Beatles – being chased – are practically suspended above ground and about to be airborne. This *overt action* sketch is the direct opposite of the implied action shot from *Reign over Me*.

IMPLIED ACTION: An image with no movement but the unspoken concept of movement. For example, a killer threatens a victim with a loaded gun.

OVERT ACTION: An image with specific movement to convey the point in the story. For example, the killer extends his arm and shoots the victim.

**Figure 7-4 Sketch from *Reign over Me*, an example of implied action.**

**Figure 7-5 Sketch of *A Hard Day's Night*, an example of overt action.**

Figure 7-6 shows a complete storyboard sequence taken from a student film that I directed when I taught film at Notre Dame. It is one of my early attempts at storyboarding, and though the idea sketches are on the crude side, they are indications of where I wanted the actors to move, utilizing directional arrows to point out that movement. Keep in mind that the concept is what counts and even these preliminary idea sketches eventually helped to make the shots as indicated. Boldness and simplicity of execution will make the point quicker than overly elaborate drawings. The storyline is simple – the Everyman character is being accosted by Death as he walks to his home through the woods.

Frame 1. Long shot of Everyman walking through the woods.

Frame 2. Medium close-up of the Death figure.

Frame 3. *The Seventh Seal* sketch.

Frame 4. Close-up of the frightened man.

Frame 5. Man falls after being touched by the Death figure.

Frame 6. Death figure continues on his way in a long shot. Note the use of arrows to indicate the movement of the figure out of the frame.

In the storyboard in Figure 7-6, I tried to keep strong, simple design elements working for me. You will note the use of foreground framing in every shot, either with the trees in frames 2, 3 and 6 and the Death figure in frames 3, 4 and 5. The black figure is combined with the trees in 1, 2, 3 and 6. Only two close-ups were used – frames 2 and 4 – for maximum impact. Note that in each of the frames, the center of interest is never placed in the center of the frame, but off-center for a strong design. The drawings themselves have been kept simple but effective in their rendering of the moving figure within its given space.

While I was the director-teacher on the shooting of this satirical short subject, I appointed a student director of photography. His job was pretty simple since we were using only winter's available light and took advantage of a built-in light metering system. We did not need to carry reflectors with us, because the snow makes for terrific reflections and fill for shadows. Since the budget on this production was minimal, covering only the cost of film and processing, I did the editing in the camera because I wasn't sure that an editor would be available. Costumes were the day-to-day apparel of the students. We made it a contemporary scenario to avoid the use of medieval costumes. The death figure's costume I borrowed from our recent production of *Hamlet* – a flowing black robe adorned with a large white cross on the chest and sporting an impressive black hood that would hide the face of the actor until his important close-up.

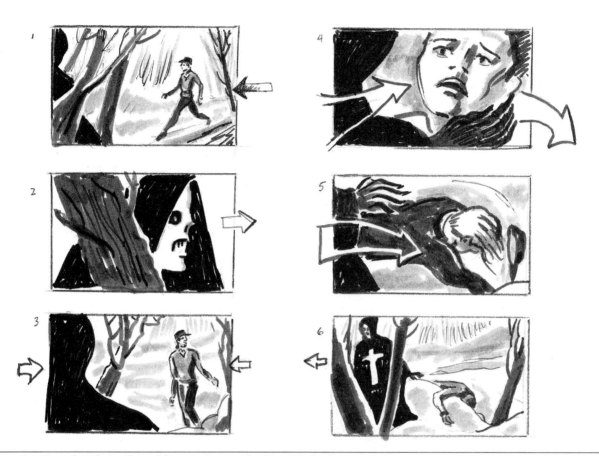

**Figure 7-6 Completed storyboard for a satire on *The Seventh Seal*.**

Our small film crew worked quickly and efficiently in the cold snow. It was so cold out there that I was afraid our borrowed Bolex with its wide angle, medium and long lenses would freeze up. When shown to the film department, the piece was appreciated as an exercise in simple film technique and production. My primitive but useful storyboard helped the director and entire student crew with the shooting of our film.

Figure 7-7 which shows great design and composition is taken from the storyboard concept and used in the eventual shot taken from the film itself. Arrows indicate the kinetic action in this pyrotechnic SFX frame. The actors are running from the car explosion. Their action has been framed off-center. A 3D quality has been achieved by the lead characters bolting quickly into the FGD, and the car (in one-point perspective) in the MGD with the flames in the BGD. In this rendering, I have given the sprinting figures the full-dimensional treatment. The wrinkling and shifting of their clothes implies the speed with which they are moving to escape from explosion.

**Figure 7-7 The storyboard concept from *The Peacemaker* (1997) demonstrates the visceral thrust into the foreground along with good framing and strong dimensional development.**

The shot in Figure 7-8 from *Citizen Kane* (1941), directed by Orson Welles, is another superb example of the combination of several action and story elements into one shot. The mother is placed in the FGD, signing the papers that will take her son away. The lawyer is just behind her. The father is in the MGD, next to the open windows. The son is seen through the window in the far BGD as he throws a snowball at the window. I have tried to show the light and shadows that are falling on the figures in a strong yet simple way using a felt-tipped pen for the chiaroscuro effect. Intense, elemental compositional devices are at work here. The figures are placed strongly in the frame but project the narrative action fulfilling the wishes of the director, the cinematographer and the set designer.

- CITIZEN KANE '41
- /MOM • DAD • BOY
- RECEDING PLANES / FGD, MED, BGD.
- DEPTH (OF FIELD) - FIGURES RECEDE, TEN.
- OFF-CENTER FRAMING OF THIS SHOT
- NATURAL LOOKING LIGHT SOURCES
- ORSON WELLES

**Figure 7-8** *Citizen Kane* **(1941).**

In the shot from *Dr. Strangelove* (1964) in Figure 7-9, the implied action is the ominous threat of a world-wide nuclear holocaust. In order to achieve the mood, the oval is used as a solid compositional device in the suspended light fixture and the round table beneath it which are a threatening visual device that looks to crush the generals at the table beneath it. The war map, which is in the BGD with its vertical dots, projects the track of the nuclear device. The curve of the light that illuminates the table, chairs and figures in them augments the mood. Great set design and lighting give strength to the world crisis being handled in the War Room.

The action involved in the schematic drawing in Figure 7-10 concerns a terrorist who, by cell phone, is trying to detonate a bomb in a Wall Street building. This sketch is adapted from a script proposal titled "Scary." The following design elements are illustrated: the golden rectangle is divided into thirds vertically and horizontally. The main center action (or attraction) is placed in the lower right of the frame. Observe the placement of the observer or the camera's eye level/horizon line (arrow just above the flag on the left) and where the two-point perspective VP's are indicated. The VP for the basic one-point perspective is placed on the horizon line just above and to the left of the seated figure with the headphones. Also, the sun as the basic light source is causing shadows on the buildings.

DR STRANGELOVE '64, KUBRICK

gH

- CIRCLES IN PERSPECTIVE • CONCENTRIC CIRCLES
- OVERHEAD LIGHTING SOURCE.
- WIDE ANGLE LENS

**Figure 7-9 Stanley Kubrick's *Dr. Strangelove* (1964).**

Figure 7-11 shows a horizontal shot with movement from left to right within the picture plane. I have drawn the moving figures in silhouette and had to work hard to give the bodies the effect of forward movement. This is a version of *Hamlet* filmed in Russia in 1964 and the director in this shot imparted a strong sense of the recession of space with his placement of the actors played off against the buildings. The FGD curve of the hill forces the eye of the viewer to look at the black figures walking to the right of the frame in the MGD. Because of their blackness, they stand out against the grayer castle in the BGD. The director created dimensional space within the pictorial frame simply with the use of strong blacks and grays.

*Lost Horizon* (Figure 7-12), a Frank Capra masterpiece, was filmed in black and white and has one of the largest sets (constructed in full scale and in miniature) that was ever built for a Hollywood film. It was released in 1937 and earned an Academy Award for Art Direction. In this shot, the arrow indicates the emergence of the characters who had been lost in the Himalayas as they enter Shangri-La. This conveys to the audience the wonders befalling the characters who are entering this 3D mise-en-scene, created by some of the best production designers in the business. As they enter, they are framed in the FGD by jutting rocks on either side, contrasted by the

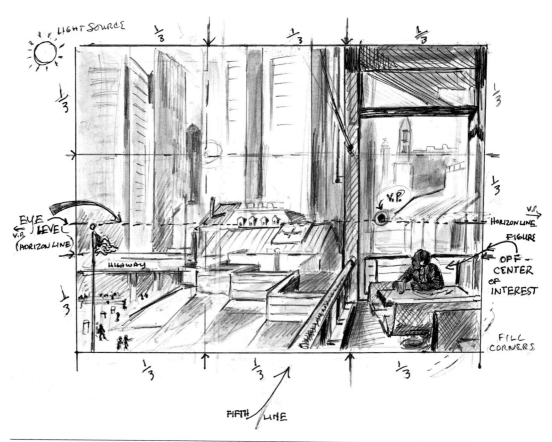

**Figure 7-10 Schematic drawing adapted for a new script.**

**Figure 7-11 *Hamlet* (1964).**

A+
• PRODUCTION DESIGN / COMPOSITION / PLANEAR
• FGD FRAMING OF FIGURES AS THEY ENTER SHANGRI-LA
• NOTE PERSPECTIVE OF POOL LINES RECEDING TO STEPS

LOST HORIZON '36
CAPRA

**Figure 7-12 *Lost Horizon* (1937).**

softer pools, gardens and the smaller figures in the MGD, while the impressive simplicity of the main buildings loom up in the BGD. The director and his team had, indeed, created visual magic which helped motivate all the characters to fulfill the destinies put forward in the script.

Zack Snyder's *300* opened in Greece in 2007 to great audience acclaim and is a jaw-dropping, visceral, visual experience, from concept art drawn in comic book style to filming actors against bluescreen/greenscreen with backgrounds digitally enhanced with CGI throughout the film. In the interpretive sketch in Figure 7-13, arrows indicate the actor's dynamic action. A groundbreaking experience indeed!

The following two examples are storyboards executed by John Tartaglione. The styles dictated by the subject matter are slightly different. Figures 7-14 through 7-16 show a storyboard from the proposed film comedy *Anything for a Laugh*. In storyboarding this sequence of the screenplay, John has given each shot what he feels will best

**Figure 7-13** *300* **(2007).**

convey the action of the story line. You can follow the narrative in frames 1 through 20.

These characters have been drawn in a simple style that lets them convey action very directly (indicated below each frame). I think that the artist has arranged the characters in interesting ways. Sometimes they are in a close-up in the FGD, at other times (as in frame 7) running horizontally through the kitchen in the MGD. Jackie chases Tom and Anthony with a baseball bat, threatening mayhem through several sets and in and out of houses. The houses are not elaborately drawn, but you know where you are.

Arrows indicate the main direction of the characters. Sometimes the storyboard artist will alternate the right-to-left action as in frame 10, with left-to-right action in frame 13. The artist has also added variety by placing the secondary character in the FGD in frame 10, then indicating the secondary character in the BGD in frame 13. Do you think that it is too much of a jump cut from frame 15 to 16? If so, draw one that you feel might work better, but try to keep it in the present style.

**Figure 7-14 *Anything for a Laugh* (1998) storyboard frames 1 through 8 (reprinted with permission from John Tartaglione).**

**Figure 7-15** *Anything for a Laugh* (1998) storyboard frames 9 through 16 (reprinted with permission from John Tartaglione).

**Figure 7-16 _Anything for a Laugh_ (1998) storyboard frames 17 through 20 (reprinted with permission from John Tartaglione).**

John has kept the use of close-ups to a minimum because there is so much body action. Saving the close-ups for a very dramatic purpose, as in frame 20, makes this technique more effective. The artist has achieved, in a very direct way, a visualization of the action of the script. With his storyboard visuals, he has also graphically shown us where the characters are going, what their motivations are and how they fulfill the intended action of the narrative.

In Figures 7-17 and 7-18, John has interpreted and rendered a sequence from John Ford's epic western _Stagecoach_ (1939) in a different style. He uses a graphite pencil, stronger blacks and whites for more contrast, more dynamic close-ups from the narrative and stronger lines. Perhaps his style has advanced from the storyboard of _Anything for a Laugh_. Perhaps the impact of an Indian attack in which one of the characters might find it necessary to shoot the women motivated him to render his images in a stronger, bolder style. Following the narrative flow of _Stagecoach_ is not difficult. The intent of both the antagonists (Indians) and the protagonists (John Wayne and the passengers) is obvious – kill or be killed – and the tension mounts until the U.S. Calvary arrives to save the day.

**Figure 7-17** *Stagecoach* **(1939) storyboard frames 1 through 6 by John Tartaglione.**

**Figure 7-18** *Stagecoach* (1939) storyboard frames 7 through 12 by John Tartaglione.

Notice how the various cuts from medium shots in frames 1 and 2 to the dramatic long shots of the attacking Indians are used. As in any Ford film, we are made to identify with the emotions of his characters in a very big way as with the device of "the other woman" trying to protect the baby in frames 2, 5 and 6. Notice also the FGD and the BGD combinations in the same frames. The Indians are alternated by the director to be seen in the BGD in 2, then used in a menacing medium shot in 3, then back to a long shot in 4. Frames 7, 8 and 9 are contrasted to the other shots because they are tight close-ups pointing in a more explicit way to the predicament of the baby, the supposed assassin and the terrified mother. Frames 10 and 11 continue in close-up with the gambler raising the gun to firing position until the quick cut to the cavalry trumpet. Strong images from a legendary director and a storyboard illustrated in the same graphic style complement the intensity of the action and the raw emotions of the characters who have been thrown into a desperate situation.

## Tutorials

1. Do a dozen quick sketches of figures in motion, starting with stick figures.

2. Add the dimension of light and shade, paying particular attention to the light sources and the resulting shadows.

# Chapter 8

## Light Sources and Depth of Field

Almost every sketch in this book shows a light source and its resultant depth of field. The light source is indicated with the symbol of a glowing sun or circle and the depth of field through graphic illustration of receding planes, i.e., the use of the FGD, MGD, and BGD. Sharper focus will occur on the center of interest (usually human figures) when the amount of light falling on the figures is more or less intense (lit by the sun, the moon or artificial light). The type of lens used to focus on the subject will also make a difference, whether it's a wide-angle lens for sharper focus or a normal lens for average sharpness.

### LIGHT SOURCES

When drawing the storyboard and interpreting any given script, the storyboard artist must always be aware of all of the indicated light sources, especially the key light, fill light, hair light or the reflected light, as well as actors' blocking and position of props. Varying the intensity of the light in your storyboard frames adds visual appeal and depth to your drawings.

The key light is most often used in the CU, and it is the main source of light that falls on the actor. This type of light can be either harsh (not diffused) or soft (*diffused* by material placed over the light source or the camera lens itself).

You'll probably want to add one or two hair lights placed behind and above the actor. The main function of a hair light is to enhance the actor's hair, especially that of a woman, and also to separate the performer from the background. The background itself is usually lit by selected area lighting done in a way that does not distract from the actors in the scene.

DIFFUSED LIGHT: Light that is softened as it passes through a filter on either the camera lens or the light itself.

Most film images are enhanced to some degree with the use of a fill light, which is simply light reflected by a rectangular white or aluminum board. The reflected light (bounced light) is directed toward the actor's face or figure. Fill light is used also to soften facial shadows. Reflected light can come from either a natural source (the sun) or an artificial light (tungsten studio lights). Fill light can also be a small spotlight or eye light positioned just below the performer's face, the camera lens and the key light. These three supplemental lighting terms all refer to any extra light source that fills shadows and softens the lighting on a face, thus giving the facial features a more flattering appearance, particularly in a CU.

My favorite lighting situation is to photograph faces outside. If the actor's back is to the sun, either mid-morning or mid-afternoon, when the sun is not directly overhead, the sun becomes the hair light/backlight falling on the actor. All you have to do is hold up a white board at the correct angle so the reflected light from the sun bounces off the white reflector onto the actor's face. See Figure 8-1.

In Figures 8-2 and 8-3, the boy's father is holding the reflector (key light) at a 45-degree angle to the sun, thus catching its light and bouncing it onto the boy's running

**Figure 8-1 A medium close-up of a young boy holding a white reflector.**

**Figure 8-2 Diagram sketch of Dad holding the reflector for his son running toward the camera.**

figure. To utilize depth of field, the photographer focuses his long lens on the leaf placed on the grass in the MGD. When the boy runs over the leaf, his running figure is in the correct MGD focal plane. The FGD plane and the BGD plane are out of focus (Figure 8-3).

In Figure 8-4, my film cinematography class is shooting an actress in outside lighting. Notice that not only do we have the model (at far left) leaning on a white reflector, but one of the students is also holding an aluminum reflector for extra bounce, or fill light on the actress' face. Naturally they are focusing on the eyes, and the BGD is out of focus. This is a suitable lighting situation for still or film.

This same technique is used in studio lighting, using either a reflector placed out of camera range (the lens' field of vision) or, in most cases, using a smaller fill light focused on the actor just below the key light (Figure 8-5).

To determine the intensity of the light, think about how close to the actors you want the light source to be. In most cases, the minimum distance is five or six feet. A key

**Figure 8-3 Photograph of the scene; notice the leaf where the lens was focused.**

light can be hard or soft. Outside, the sun can be the key light, or at least the source for reflected light. Most film images are diffused to some degree and the use of a fill light softens the facial shadows. In Figure 8-6, a studio MCU of Stephanie Danielson's face, the key light effect is soft and the hair light is angled down to illuminate the back and sides of her head and enhance her hair. The hair light can be as soft or as intense as you prefer and is usually one-third as strong as the key light.

In Figure 8-7, the key light illuminates Kathleen Richard's face, the backlight highlights the hair, and a fill light bounces into the shadows of the face to soften the shadow caused by the key light. (This time, the fill light was a large scoop light softened with diffusion material.) Also, an eye light is placed directly in front of her face to give her eyes a lively highlight. This is "star" lighting that the extras don't get – they are lit with area lighting, a general expanded light that lets them be seen, but doesn't emphasize any special features. A few examples follow later using analytical sketches taken from certain shots from classic films which will define these lighting and compositional concepts further. Figure 8-8 is the *lighting plot* for a portrait shot.

LIGHTING PLOT: Correct placement of lights for the actors and the scenes in which they appear.

HART NYU FILM CLASS
    WITH    REFLECTORS
            ON MODEL

STEPHANIE'S
    C.U.

**Figure 8-4 Cinematography class shooting outside, and the resulting shot.**

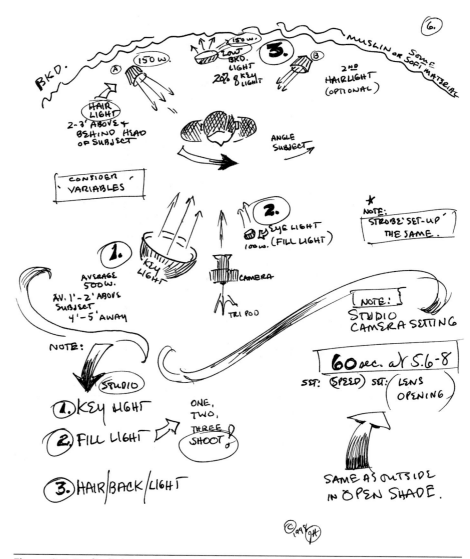

**Figure 8-5 Studio lighting diagram from Hart's booklet "chalk talks," explanatory illustrations for his photography class at NYU.**

As the storyboard artist collaborating with the director of photography or cinematographer who is in charge of creating the lighting moods and atmosphere that reflect the director's vision and intent, you must be familiar with the lighting and compositional tools that might be discussed in the preproduction meetings. They will expect you to be familiar with most of the basic terms that pertain to lighting, lenses

**Figure 8-6 MCU photograph shot in the studio with a soft key light and downward-angled hair light.**

and camera angles so you can interpret exactly what they want and illustrate the effects of the lighting plots in your storyboard. For the same reason, you must have some knowledge of lenses used in the filming, such as normal lens (MS – medium shot), long lens (LS – long shot) or wide angle lens.

## DEPTH OF FIELD

*Depth of field* refers to the point in the image where you want the sharpest focus. This might be a person or an object, and it might be in the FGD, MGD or BGD. This place of sharpest focus is the place of greatest interest in the shot. For many people, depth of field is difficult to visualize. To me the term depth of field has always been a misnomer.

For clarity let's use the farm world as a reference point.

What depth?

The depth of the well in the back of the house?

DEPTH OF FIELD: The area of the shot that is in sharpest focus, indicating the area of greatest interest.

**Figure 8-7 Studio portrait shot with "star" lighting for maximum effect and emphasis.**

The depth of the pile of compost in front of cow barn?

What field?

That field with the cows outside the farmer's window?

That field that Gramps refers to as the North 40?

Well, yes and no to all of the above. Whoever came up with the term depth of field was referring to our human field of vision – what our retinas and optic nerves can absorb (light rays) when we view any given scene.

On our farm location, how much depth has that field of grass? Its depth is the distance from where we, the viewers, stand and the space that stretches from FGD to MGD to BGD. In this sketch, the viewing field of vision encompasses the distance from the front fence all the way back to the row of trees in the back of the field – maybe half a mile away from us.

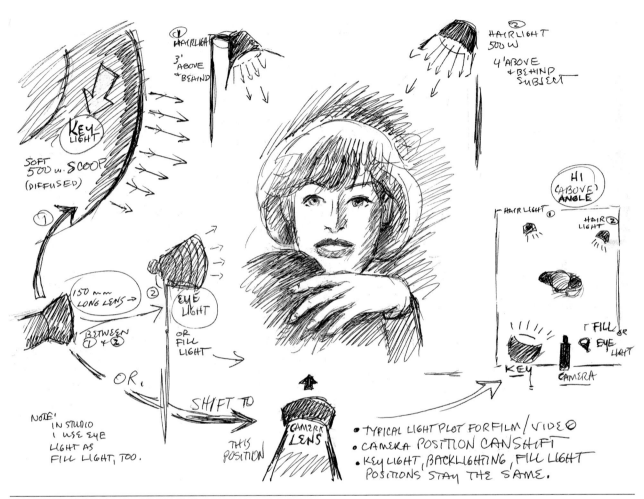

**Figure 8-8 Light plot for Figure 8-7.**

Depth of field does not refer to the height of the grass in the field. We have discussed receding planes: FGD, MGD and BGD, and the required center of interest for every shot. First, if that fence framing the field in front of our view is in the FGD, then the grazing cow occupies the MGD. Second, that row of trees behind Nellie occupies the BGD. Third, keeping the cow in focus is our main concern because she is our center of interest. We're not interested in the FGD fence, or the trees in the BGD. We will focus our lens, probably a long lens, only on the cow. Our bovine friend will be in focus more sharply than that FGD fence or the BGD row of trees.

Also, if we focus on Nellie with our long lens, the BGD will automatically go out of focus because the long lens has limited the depth of field. (Note the bird's-eye view in Figure 8-9.)

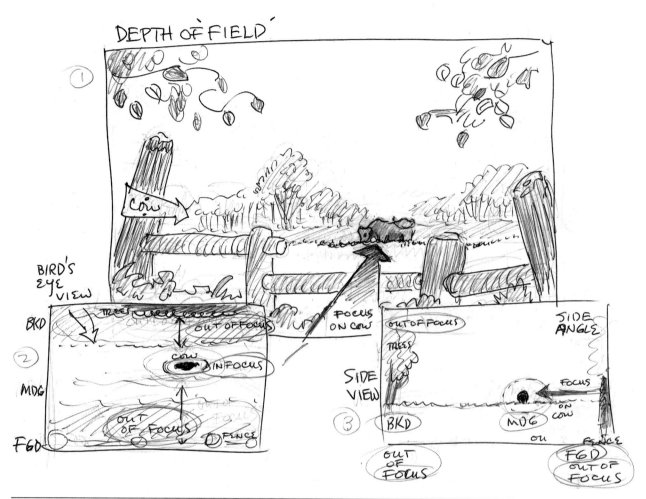

**Figure 8-9 A farm scene sketch illustrating depth of field.**

If it's a bright, sunny day, the depth of field will increase, so the grass just in front of Nellie and the grass directly behind her will be more in focus too, i.e., in the MGD focal plane. Why? Brighter light causes your aperture to close down a stop or two, increasing the depth of field. Optics again! Light increases the depth of field.

If Nellie walks up to us into the FGD, focusing on her will be easier. On a professional film shoot, there will be a *focus puller*, whose only job is to follow focus while adjusting the lens, making sure that Nellie is constantly in focus as she moves from MGD to FGD.

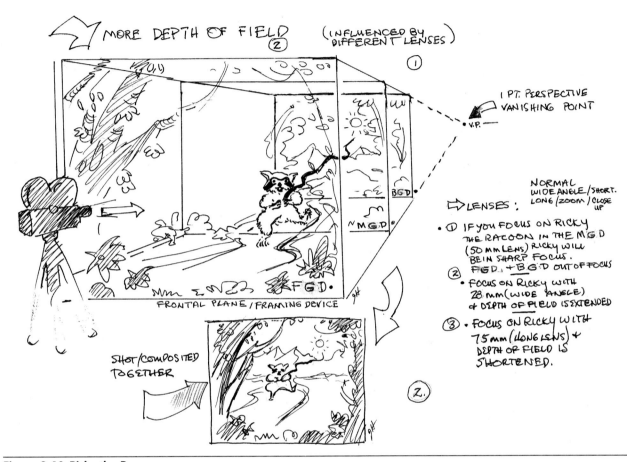

**Figure 8-10 Ricky the Raccoon.**

Depth of field is the distance selected in your field of vision for proper focus. Figures 8-10 and 8-11 show more examples and explanations of depth of field.

Figure 8-12 is a shot of my sketching class in the FGD of the World Trade Center's Heaven's Gate solarium. They are drawing the room's perspective from their point of view. Note the bold geometric design of the interior.

Who is in the MGD?

What is in the BGD?

Where is the main light source?

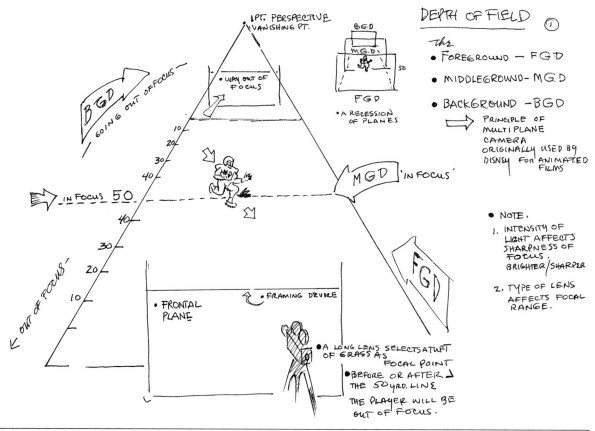

**Figure 8-11 Football analogy.**

## CLASSIC FILM EXAMPLES

Figure 8-13 is a sketch taken from *The Birth of a Nation* (1915), D. W. Griffith's landmark film about the Civil War. It elevated movies into an art form and was the most famous film until *Gone with the Wind* in 1939. Photographed by his indispensable cinematographer, Billy Bitzer, this scene is a tableau permeated with natural sunlight that is the main light source, taken from the Southern point of view. Normally, this is not the time of day for a shoot because of the harsh overhead shadows, but it works here to add raw realism, sharp detail and focus. Because of the strong lighting, the depth of field is not only very sharp, but also extends beyond the soldiers in the FGD.

William Daniels, the cinematographer Greta Garbo demanded on all her films, backlit Garbo in many scenes, giving her hair a halo of luminosity, then lit her

**Figure 8-12 My sketching class at the WTC.**

**Figure 8-13 Dramatic scene from *The Birth of a Nation*.**

GRAND HOTEL '32  AA BEST PICTURE - GARBO/BARRYMORE
STRONG BACKLIGHT/HAIRLIGHT
SOFTER KEY LIGHT (DIFFUSED) ON FACES

**Figure 8-14 Greta Garbo and John Barrymore in Grand Hotel (1932).**

famous bone structure with a soft, diffused, romantic key light. He added another soft fill light to soften the shadows (Figure 8-14).

Figure 8-15 shows a shot from *Citizen Kane* (1941), directed by Orson Welles and photographed by Gregg Toland. Their close collaboration produced a film that is invariably at the top of everyone's "10 best films of all time" list. Kane's key light is hitting him at a 45-degree angle but has been manipulated to shade his face from the eyes to the top of his head, creating the emotional mood of a man whose life is spent. He is being blocked out, shaded and pressed in upon. The focus is specifically on Kane, using a normal lens in a MCU, causing the shadows from the beams in the ceiling behind him to eventually soften as they recede in perspective. Shot from an unnervingly low angle, it photographs him almost silhouetted against those receding rafters, in turn reflecting his diminishing power.

Figure 8-16 exudes high drama, a sketch from *Ivan the Terrible, Part II* (1958). A strong *chiaroscuro* effect is caused by the intense key light emanating from the left. It is an original composition that is strong from the FGD figures to the MGD shadow of Ivan, all the way to the tapestry in the BGD. The great depth of field comes from the brilliant key lighting along with supplemental lighting in the rear throne area.

CHIAROSCURO: High contrast light and shade, as in film noir.

RECEDING HORIZONTALS OF BED CEILING
STRONG OVERHEAD LIGHTING SOURCE

CITIZEN KANE '41

**Figure 8-15 An analytical sketch from *Citizen Kane*.**

• ARCHITECTONIC FRAMING
STRONG LIGHT + SHADE

IVAN THE TERRIBLE II
EISENSTEIN.
TISSE

**Figure 8-16 Analytical lighting sketch from *Ivan the Terrible, Part II*.**

*DR. ZHIVAGO '65
LEAN
AA TO FREDDIE FIELDS, CINEMATOGRAPHY
&ART DIRECTION — JOHN BOX.

**Figure 8-17 An analytical sketch of *Doctor Zhivago*.**

Figure 8-17 is my water color rendering of a scene from *Doctor Zhivago* (1965). A scene that helped Freddie Young, the director of photography and John Box, production designer, win Academy Awards for their visual contributions to this stunning film. This illustration is a night scene permeated with an ethereal blue that floods the residence. Compositionally, the horizontal shadows in the FGD contrast with the vertical trees within the same plane. The strongest light source is from the left, with a strong overhead sky lighting descending on the snow-covered house and grounds. This lighting, along with the wide angle Panavision lens, creates a deeper depth of field.

In 1982, Stephen Spielberg's *E.T.* was a ground-breaking venture in fantasy science fiction using animatronics along with real actors. E.T.'s movements were more believable than anything ever before. Even in Figure 8-18, you can see why he looked so real – the same glamour lighting used on Garbo was used on E.T. E.T. and the boy were backlit, while a soft, flattering key light emanated from the glow of his index finger. A general fill light surrounds the alien so E.T. and the boy are equals.

In the interpretive sketch of a shot from *Forrest Gump* (1994) in Figure 8-19, the use of one-point perspective is obvious. Figure 8-20 is an example of forced per-

AA/VISUAL EFFECTS / VERY STRONG BACKLIGHTING,                    E.T. '82

**Figure 8-18 An analytical sketch from *E.T.***

RSALITY
FULL
SIZE
HOUSE

FORREST
GUMP
'94

1 PT. PERSP.

OFF CENTER
FIGURES
+ HOUSE

LOOK FOR
CENTER LINE
OF FIGURE

KEEP COMPARING
ONE FORM TO ANOTHER
- HEAD TO HIPS, ETC

STICK FIGURE
FIRST IN PENCIL

OVERLAY WITH
PEN + INK

**Figure 8-19 *Forrest Gump* one-point perspective.**

**Figure 8-20** *Forrest Gump* **forced perspective.**

spective, where the wall to the right is made larger in the FGD and forced to appear smaller by the time it reaches the MGD. The house in the BGD is one-tenth the size of a real house, so you have compressed a scene from FGD to BGD, and this adds to the fairy tale feel of the setting. Figure 8-20 has added a sense of surrealism or unreality to the scene. Forced perspective has been demonstrated in previous chapters, particularly in *James and the Giant Peach* in Figure 2-14.

*Giant* (1956), starring Elizabeth Taylor and Rock Hudson, featured James Dean, one of the icons of the 20th century. Boris Leven's superb visual interpretation of the scenario won him a nomination for an Academy Award for Art Direction. Figure 8-21 shows Dean as the FGD framing and the ranch house in the BGD. The ranch house is as strongly lit as the foreground because of the intense sunlight, creating a greater depth of field.

As always, I recommend that you always carry a small sketchbook and take a few moments to record images or scenes that you find interesting. These "quickies" help you think quickly and will help when you have to come up with fast concept sketches in script sessions with directors. These sketches, along with others you have seen in this text, are graphic examples of what the storyboard artist-to-be should be doing in his or her spare time. These rough sketches can always be rendered in a more finished way later, but in the meantime they assist you in becoming a more facile

DEPTH OF FIELD
FORGROUND FRAMING / PRODUCTION DESIGN

JAMES DEAN
STEVENS   GIANT '55

**Figure 8-21 Interpretive sketch for *Giant*.**

artist who is adept at proportion, composition, lighting and placement of figures in the mise-en-scene of the shot. It is the job of a good storyboard artist to design each frame so the center of interest in each scene is maintained using strong compositional devices. Extraneous elements that distract should be avoided. It is most important that you that you learn how to think and draw three-dimensionally.

| Tutorials |
| --- |

1. Select 12 examples of photos from magazines, film stills or newspapers that indicate various depths of field and light sources.

2. Make a simple sketch of each, noting the FGD, MGD and BGD, and add light and shade to each sketch.

# Chapter 9

## The Shot, Its Dynamics and Its Function in the Storyboard

The visual language of cinema is a language of story structure whose grammar is made up of "the shot." The storyboard is a series of illustrated shots. To paraphrase Gertrude Stein, "a shot is a shot is a shot." Like Stein's poetry, the shot has its own simplicity and its own complexities, its hard realities and its emotional side. The director has to figure out exactly what he or she wants the shot to say to the audience. By way of introduction to the variables and components of the shot and why it is the visual heart of the movie-making process, let's go back to the audience itself. The audience's attention must be grabbed by the shot or a succession of shots that make up the storyline.

Everyday you hear people with cameras saying, "I want to get a shot of you" or "Let me get a shot of the Parthenon before we go back to the hotel." This is "the shot" that focuses on a particular scene taken with your camera to capture it on film.

The difference in making films is that a series of shots of a particular scene are taken – motivated by events specifically drawn from the written screenplay or script. Film is foremost an artistic medium that desires an emotional response from its audience. The audience must be treated with respect. Preproduction storyboarding is a must to create a film with a strong story line, one that will visually interpret the written words of the screenwriter, one that the audience will enjoy. B. P. Schulberg, production head of Paramount Pictures in the golden age of Hollywood, told one of his production teams, "We don't have to waste time hammering out a story line. What you do is visualize it; think of every scene (shot) as the camera will see it, not as you would describe it in prose."

Any series of shots has to be part of the story structure, and it has to make up an entertainment package. Sergei Eisenstein compressed the entire Russian Revolution into 75 shots for the *Battleship Potemkin* (see Chapter 6). He was continually experimenting with different combinations of shots in his striving for artistic perfection.

Figure 9-1 is my diagrammatic illustration of the structural make-up of a storyboard. A storyboard is composed of a series of shots that will be photographed in sequence following the continuity of the script. Illustrating this series (frames) in a logical, structural rhythm is the job of the storyboard artist. The shots themselves have to have stunning, eye-pleasing content. Since the shot itself is the smallest element that

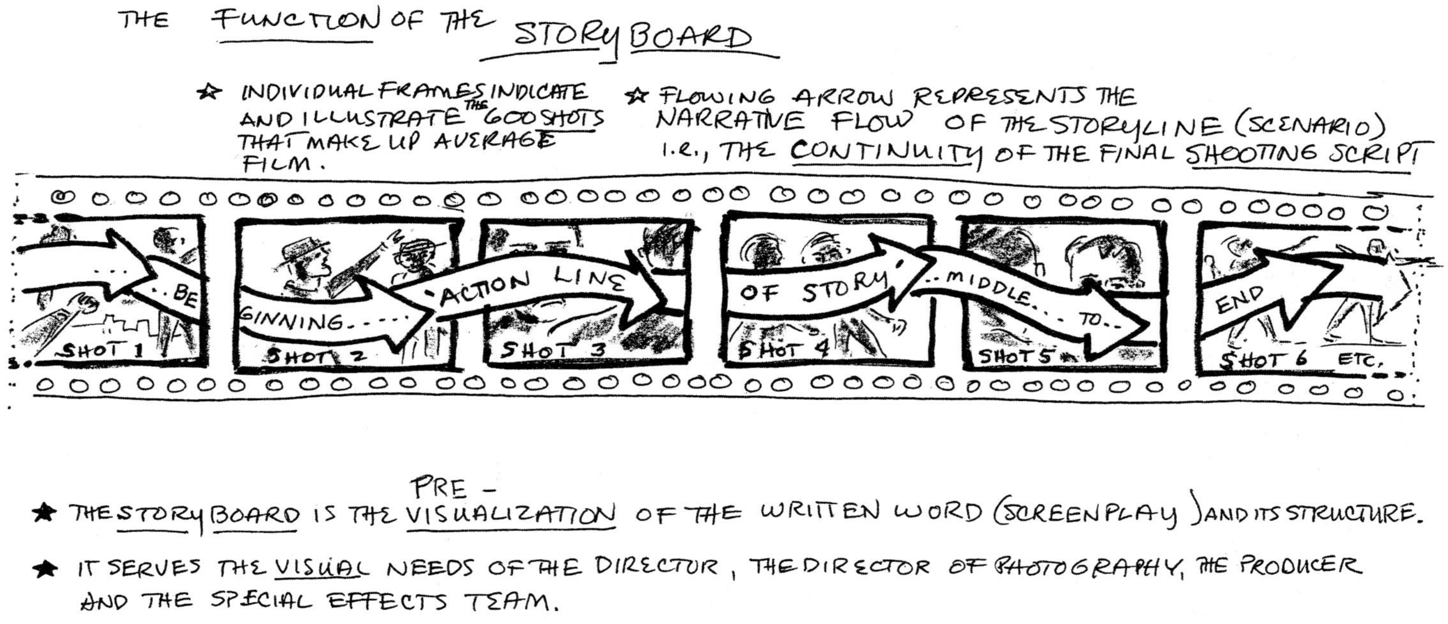

THE FUNCTION OF THE STORYBOARD

☆ INDIVIDUAL FRAMES INDICATE AND ILLUSTRATE THE GOOD SHOTS THAT MAKE UP AVERAGE FILM.

☆ FLOWING ARROW REPRESENTS THE NARRATIVE FLOW OF THE STORYLINE (SCENARIO) i.e., THE CONTINUITY OF THE FINAL SHOOTING SCRIPT

BEGINNING — ACTION LINE — MIDDLE — OF STORY — TO — END — ETC.

SHOT 1   SHOT 2   SHOT 3   SHOT 4   SHOT 5   SHOT 6

★ THE STORYBOARD IS THE VISUALIZATION OF THE WRITTEN WORD (SCREENPLAY) AND ITS STRUCTURE. PRE-

★ IT SERVES THE VISUAL NEEDS OF THE DIRECTOR, THE DIRECTOR OF PHOTOGRAPHY, THE PRODUCER AND THE SPECIAL EFFECTS TEAM.

**Figure 9-1 The function of a storyboard.**

makes up the film scenario, it dictates its own psychological, artistic and intellectual demands. The shots should have a unity of action and must obey a certain principle of order.

**In "The Film Experience," Roy Huss and Norman Silverstein state, "The storyboard artist, guided by the director, captures the action and passions that will be translated into film. Even though his series of drawings is accompanied by written actions and dialogue, the continuity reminiscent of action comic strips remains primarily pictorial."**

Figure 9-2 is an effective atmospheric shot from *Duel in the Sun* (1946), produced by David Selznick, with no obvious linear perspective, only a LS (long shot) of the figures silhouetted against a setting sun. The Earth is part of the darker FGD plane and the night sky acts as the BGD plane. The use of circles is a strong design element. Observe the one-third/two-thirds division of Earth and sky.

The primary questions that one has to ask in reference to the content of the shot are these:

- What are the demands of the script?

- Who is involved in the scene?

- In what locale do these characters exist?

- Why are they there?

- What mood will enhance the setup of this particular shot? What colors will augment the emotions involved in the conflict?

- Where will the camera be placed to best advantage? What lenses will be used for establishing the shot?

In a memorable series of shots from Alfred Hitchcock's infamous *Psycho* (1960), shown in Figure 9-3, note the original way he filmed this action, with the use of a stunning variety of angles to set the mood and enhance the suspense.

Frame 1. A CU of the back of Anthony Perkins' head and an EST SHOT to let us know where the action actually takes place.

Frame 2. Cut to CU of the side of Perkins' head as he looks through a peep hole.

Frame 3. Cut to MS of Janet Leigh, undressing.

Frame 4. Cut to EXT CU of Perkins' eye, staring.

Frame 5. Cut to MS of Leigh continuing to undress.

GOLDEN MEAN AT WORK
CIRCLES/DESIGN
SETTING SUN AS LIGHT SOURCE

DUEL IN THE SUN '47

**Figure 9-2 *Duel in the Sun* (1946).**

Frame 6.  Cut to Low Angle MS of Leigh under shower head.

Frame 7.  Cut to Low Angle of showerhead.

Frame 8.  Cut to MS of Leigh's profile under shower head.

Frame 9.  Cut to Leigh, three-quarter MS, right of frame.

Frame 10.  Cut to MS of Perkins, through shower with knife.

Frame 11.  Cut to CU, Perkins' hand with knife.

**Figure 9-3 Storyboard for the *Psycho* shower scene.**

Frame 12. Cut to CU, Leigh screaming.

Frame 13. Cut to EXT CU, Leigh's mouth.

Frame 14. Cut to MS, Leigh grabs Perkins' arm.

Frame 15. Cut to EXT CU, knife at her midsection.

Frame 16. Cut to tight CU, Leigh's face.

These graphic shots from one of the best-ever suspense films illustrates the brilliant use of diverse camera angles which – combined with Bernard Herrmann's eerie score and Hitchcock's incisive editing – create a truly frightening sequence.

The next two sketches are interpretations of what you might be doing after a discussion with the director or author about a new script concept. The drawings done quickly at a first meeting might be fleshed out and discussed as a storyboard concept at the next meeting. This is a sample of a page from Jeff Chena's new script; the working title is *The Last Ten Yards*. In this shot, psychic fortune teller Madame Zena reads some terrifying cards, predicting some bad news for the male lead, who is a famous football player (see Figure 9-4).

Figure 9-5 is another page from this script showing a flashback CU shot of our hero's eyes as he is about to be killed by a Knights Templar. The arrow indicates transition to the second shot, where Madame Zena reacts to her vision of his murder.

Many variables indeed are involved in the content of the shot, and the storyboard artist's familiarity with them certainly will be of inestimable use for the entire creative team. The sequence of shots cannot be static. The story line has to move. The individual shots have to flow like music. They need a rhythm of their own. They must be paced so as to follow one another with appropriate speed. For instance, how long should the camera hold on any one shot?

You can't hold on to the scene as though it were a painting, because the scene has to keep moving so the audience is glued to the screen. The audience must have its share of kinetic thrills, experience the planned unity of action, emotion and environment of each shot as the moving pictures continue to flow along with the continuity of the script.

*Citizen Kane* (1941) is required viewing for any film student. Figure 9-6 shows a high angle shot of Orson Welles doing the final lining up of a shot, with his legendary cinematographer Gregg Toland. See this film just for its superb handling of a fluid camera, its extremely sharp depth of field (wide angle lens plus extra lights on BGD), its use of compositing (putting several separately photographed shots into one frame), its original use of camera angles, and its legendary story line.

The series of shots should result in a cumulative action that imparts a fully realized look to the film itself. Wherever the scene takes place, each shot contains certain production details that have been selected for inclusion in the storyboard. No extraneous details should be included, only those that pertain to the here and now of the story being told. Professionals make these selections ahead of time, and the storyboard artist is on hand, helping translate the director's vision in deciding which elements of the scene will be selected and designed with camera placement, choice of lenses, and compositional framing in mind.

Robert Duncan of Duncan Films came to me recently to help him with concept sketches and storyboards for *Fu Project*, a project they are filming for the Chinese Educational System. It is a series of films that will help students become familiar with

stare.

The knight lifts the sword and begins to swing. The wounded
knight closes his eyes. He cries out in pain.

CUT TO:

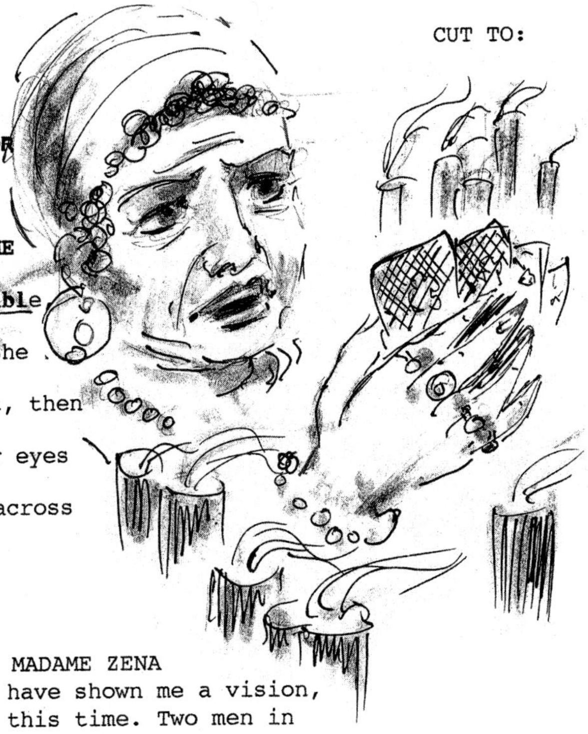

INT.DAY.PSYCHICS PARLOR

In a dark gloomy room,

Candles Burning, **MADAME**

**ZENA 60's** sits At a table

her eyes are closed, She

jolts back in her seat, then

Cries out in pain. Her eyes

Open Wide. She looks across

the table.

           MADAME ZENA
    The spirits have shown me a vision,
    it's not of this time. Two men in
    armor fighting to one is dead.

SONNY "THE MOOSE" FURMA, **50's, chiseled features, upcoming
Mafia chieftain,** looks at her serious.

MADAME ZENA POV: SONNY'S deadly piercing stare, the same as
the one in vision.

           MADAME ZENA
    The Same of blood.  The spirits are
    telling me..., you killed your own
    brother in a previous life.  Death is
    in the air.  Shuffle the cards again,
    break them in three piles and then
    pick a pile.

**Figure 9-4 Script page for Chena's new film with an interpretive sketch of the selected action. Courtesy of Odyssey Pictures and JL Media, Dallas, Texas, and Jeff Chena.**

COMMENTATOR (O.S.)
Spear struggling to get the ball into
the end zone. He's driven back, to
the 4 yard line. The ball flies
loose. Yardsville recovers. Another
bad break for Spear.

Yardsville players all celebrate.   Johnny lies on his back.

CLOSE-UP JOHNNY'S EYES.

DISSOLVE TO:

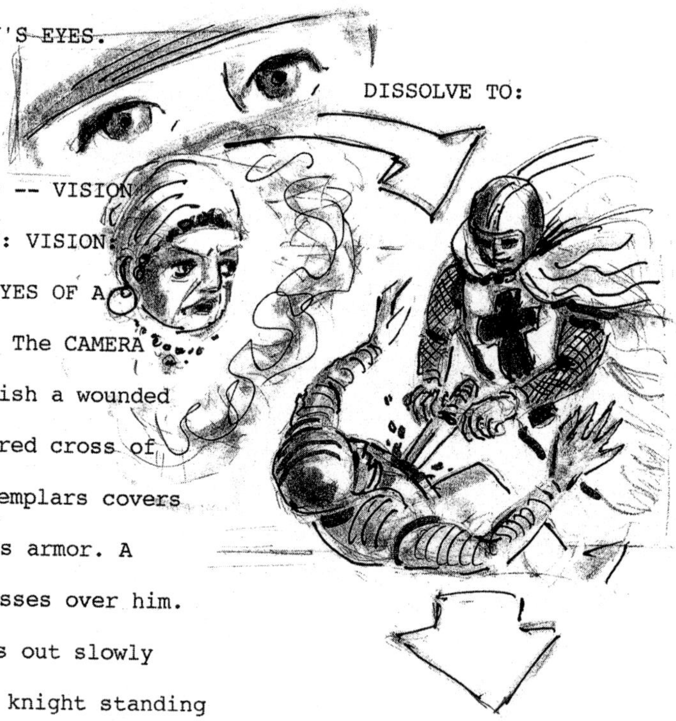

EXT. DUSK FIELD -- VISION

MADAME ZENA POV: VISION

CLOSE-UP: THE EYES OF A

WOUNDED KNIGHT. The CAMERA

Pullback establish a wounded

Knight. A huge red cross of

The Knight of Templars covers

The Front of his armor. A

huge Shadow Crosses over him.

THE CAMERA pulls out slowly

Establishing an knight standing

Over him, the knight pulls out a

sword. The wounded knight slowly

speaks.

WOUNDED KNIGHT.
We are the same blood.  Brothers,
Born of the same mother.  You
will....

WOUNDED KNIGHTS POV: The knights eye's, a deadly piercing

**Figure 9-5 Second script page for a new film with an interpretive sketch of the action. Courtesy of Odyssey Pictures and JL Media, Dallas TX and Jeff Chena.**

**Figure 9-6 Orson Welles and Gregg Toland checking a set-up for a shot.**

the history of Chinese characters (lettering). Figure 9-7 shows concept sketches provided by the director. My job was to visualize these concept sketches for him.

Figure 9-8 is a promotional piece for *Fu Project* (note text) for which three more fully realized concept sketches were chosen (one of which is enlarged in Figure 9-9).

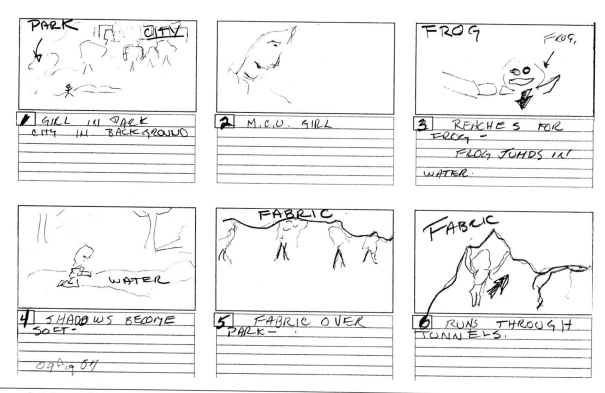

**Figure 9-7 Some of Robert Duncan's concept sketches for his selected shots.**

Left frame. INT. Night. Our young leading lady is day-dreaming in her bedroom, gazing out at the night sky.

Center frame. EXT. Day. In a park-like setting, she sees a large orange parachute descending from the sky directly in front of her.

Right frame. CU. Girl, seeing that the parachute was attached to a space capsule that has fallen into the trees, endeavors to open the escape hatch for the astronaut.

Insert box in upper righthand corner of frame, indicates a LS of the scene.

## MONTAGE

A film technique used very effectively by many directors is the montage. The definition of montage in "The Film Encyclopedia" (Ephraim Katz), as it is applied to motion pictures, is "a sequence made up of a quick succession of brief shots blending and dissolving into one another, created to compress action and convey the passage of

## Our Story: "Fu Project"

**Capitalizing on China's Excitement over it's Recent Accomplishment in SpaceExploration . . .**

- **Outline:**
  - A returning space capsule lands slightly off course
  - Our young heroine happens upon the scene and greets our astronaut
  - Three curious 'aliens' have stowed aboard
  - From a civilized planet, our friendly aliens come seeking a written form of communication
  - These cute little creatures befriend the eight year old girl who begins teaching them the Chinese characters

- **Female Lead**

- **Unique personalities and magical powers of the 'aliens' make learning fun and exciting**

- **On-going plotline divided into 5-minute connecting episodes**

- **Reflect evolution of written Chinese characters**

- **Revealing historic cultural relevance through fun and fantasy**

**Figure 9-8 The promotional piece for Fu Project, courtesy of Robert Duncan, Duncan Films.**

time." A *montage* can refer to several images overlapping each other or a series of separate images that are edited in continuity while conveying something quite different in meaning, instigating an emotional or intellectual response.

Eisenstein seems to have made montage the symbol that it has become. He employed it many times to stunning effect, but even he was influenced to a great extent by D. W. Griffith, especially as Griffith manipulated his editing in *Intolerance*

**MONTAGE:** Individual shots or images that conflict with each other (Eisenstein) arranged in a pre-viz continuity.

**Figure 9-9 Enlarged concept sketch for *Fu Project*.**

to achieve the sympathetic emotional response he wanted from the audience. The opening scenes from *Gone with the Wind* are another example of montage, introducing the audience to the culture of the Old South. It is a tableau that flows effortlessly from one shot into another creating a stunning montage.

We think of montage as the assemblage of footage to give a sequence of different shots, used as a device to satisfy the visual demands of the script created at the discretion of the director.

The director has to consider plot points like:

- Will using a montage in this particular spot advance the story line?

- Will it have the pace, metric precision, and rhythm that are needed?

- Does the script necessitate a metaphorical or intellectual message here?

- Will it wind up attracting attention to itself?

In some instances, the editing will deliver the montage effect when it is cut from the footage that has already been shot.

**Figure 9-10 Storyboard sequence from *Stagecoach*.**

Figure 9-10 is a storyboard sequence from John Ford's *Stagecoach*. Zoom shots were not used at the time this film was shot, so cuts from LS to MS to CU were part of the montage. Frame 1 is a LS, which cuts to a MS in frames 2 and 3, and then the MCU in frame 4. By frame 8, the star, John Wayne, has fallen into a series of CU shots. He has moved from BGD to MGD to the FGD planes.

Figure 9-11 is a scene from the epic *The Godfather* (1972), first of the *Godfather* trilogy. This is an interpretive sketch from a shot at the beginning of the film that illustrates implied action, off-center framing of a secondary character, strong overhead lighting and strong geometric design. This epic tale of the mafia life (and death) is often placed at the top of many of the Best American Movies list, even beating out other greats like *Citizen Kane* and *Gone With the Wind*, however it is number three on the American Film Institute's list. The film is a winner of the Academy Award for Best Picture in 1972, and Brando got Best Actor award. Director Francis Ford Coppola was nominated for an Academy Award, as was the "over-the-head" style of dark, moody lighting by Cinematographer Gordon Willis.

**Figure 9-11 Brando in a dramatic two-shot from *The Godfather*.**

In the storyboard from *The Godfather, Part I* (Figure 9-12), Francis Ford Coppola uses several different techniques to convey the meaning of this sequence. The lead character, Don Michael Corleone, is attending his son's baptism.

Frame 1. MCU of the priest's hand and the baby's head. Note: Hands are a continuing motif in this montage.

Frame 2. Cut to CU barber's hands reaching for the lather.

Frame 3. Lather is applied to the character who will later be murdered in the chair.

Frame 4. Cut back to the priest's hands during the baptism.

Frame 5. Michael (right) has ordered the execution of his competitors; on left are other witnesses to the baptism.

Frame 6. Cut to hand holding open an elevator door OTS shot of the assassin.

**Figure 9-12 Storyboard of *The Godfather, Part I*.**

Frame 7. MS, the gunman holds elevator door open and fires.

Frame 8. Quick cut to Michael at the baptism.

Frame 9. Another OTS from the opposite angle, man on a massage table.

Frame 10. MCU, wait in suspense for the execution.

Frame 11. CU of the now dead body.

Frame 12. Cut back to Michael in a tighter CU, at the baptism, but his mind is on the killings he ordered.

This Coppola montage has great visceral action with its dual story line, graphic compositions, strong framing and imaginative choice of camera angles and held together by the sound track playing organ music through the executions.

## EDITING

Although editing is an integral part of the filmmaking process, it comes at the end of that progression, almost opposite the creation of the storyboards. In other words, it is postproduction, not preproduction, although some famous directors like Alfred Hitchcock and Ridley Scott have already edited their films in the structure of their storyboards. They left no room for anyone else to interfere with the director's original vision. Ira Konigsberg said in "The Complete Film Dictionary," "It is the editor/cutter who, by shaping and arranging shots, scenes and sequences, while also modulating and integrating sound, has considerable influence in the development, rhythm, emphasis and final impact of the film."

Figure 9-13 shows a sequence from *The French Connection* (1971) where the audience experiences just one example of the brilliant editing in the film. Pacing-wise, every selected shot is held on screen for just the right length of time before a cut to the next shot. The use of too long a shot or too short a shot would break the pace, the momentum, and the rhythm of its dramatic construction. In montages, as in music, tempo must be orchestrated. On viewing this film, we are aware of a dynamic, kinetic sequence of fluid shots. The director has let us know exactly where we are, who is involved in the action and what the individual motivations are – all elements building to this climatic shot. Every shot in *The French Connection* was storyboarded.

Whether it's in a hotel room or on the Riviera, a shot of one, two, three or a dozen people, it is important that each shot contains the details that have been selected for use within the previously designed frame of reference, details that pertain to the here and now of the story. This continuity is evident in the storyboard for the screenplay *Sheriff*, Figures 9-14 and 9-15. A logical line of action is consistent with the placement of characters in each frame. There is no jumping in and out of the established sight lines. Reading from left to right, it easy to distinguish the EST shot in frame 1; the OTS in frames 4, 8, 11 and 12; MS shots in frames 4, 7, 14 and 15; ECU in frame 2 and CUs in frames 5, 6 and 10. The only LS is in frame 14 of the boat framed in the FGD by a curtain left of frame and Blake off center in profile right of frame. These storyboards were rendered with minimal pen and ink lines shaded with a felt tip pen.

Figure 9-16 is a metaphor for the awakening masses responding to the mutiny on the *Potemkin*. The three lions were actually shot from three different locations. Frame 1 is a MCU, frame 2 is a CU and frame 3 is a MS. Separately, each shot could be referred to as *mimetic* (a static imitation of life), but as combined by Eisenstein, they project kinetic vitality and spring to life. As with any shot, the length of time it is allowed to stay on the screen is up to the director who is aware of how the timing affects the pace and rhythm of the scene. The lions sequence became part of the montage of images that Eisenstein was building into the structure of the narrative.

□ ■ □ ■ □ ■ □ ■

MIMETIC: Imitative action, opposite of kinetic.

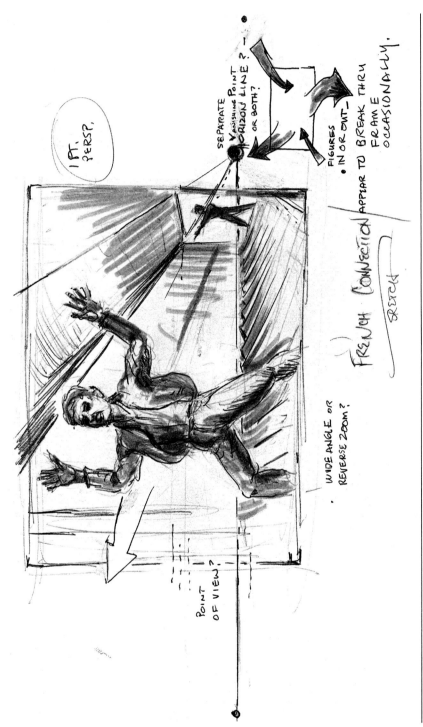

**Figure 9-13** *The French Connection.*

**Figure 9-14 An original sketch of conference scene for *Sheriff*.**

Figure 9-17's four-frame sequence from Dino So (www.dinoso.de) shows how a brief storyboard can become a finished and dramatic product as visually exciting as any of Eisenstein's shots from *Battleship Potemkin*.

Frame 1. EXT Night. Country road. CU of wrecked car careening off moving smaller red car – left of frame.

Dramatic framing of shot. Notice "action" rays emanating from smash-up. Use of Eisenstein's concept of conflict, i.e., placement of forms: large mass vs. small mass.

Frame 2. INT. Driver's POV, CU of hand at wheel of red car heading for blue car, off-center to left of frame.

Frame 3. Blue car smashes into red car. Note again the off-center play of the two forms and the dynamic action rays exploding from the broken car pieces. Strong inverted pyramid composition.

**Figure 9-15 An original sketch of conference scene for *Sheriff*, continued.**

**Figure 9-16 Three shots of the lions from *Battleship Potemkin*.**

**Figure 9-17 The four-frame storyboard sequence called *Rear Window* from artist Dino So, 2001, www.dinoso.de, www.illustrationen.de, www.storyboards.nl.**

Frame 4. LS major explosion BGD that is centered in frame but at least has dynamic movement.

Also note that all of these four storyboard frames obey the rule of thirds (see Chapter 4).

**Figure 9-18 *Disturbia* (2007).**

The 2007 film *Disturbia* emulates Hitchcock (*Rear Window*) in its composition (Figure 9-18). Design-wise, the positioning of a generous circle within a rectangle produces a very strong visual, and using two circles here makes for double whammy. Imagery, along with the added benefit of double images (the frightened girl right FGD with killer in BGD) is seen twice in the binoculars. This imagery has been used in films since the silent era right up to Hitchcock's *Rear Window* and beyond – demonstrating that voyeurism is apparently still "in." The use of the binocular image is also shown in our previous section on the use of simple stick figures in one's storyboards (Chapter 6, Figure 6-1).

## DYNAMIC DESIGN

MIT Press has recently published a fine book by Suguru Ishizaki titled "Improvisational Design," a theoretical text that confronts the new challenge of a more dynamic set of design problems involving today's communication advances. Suguru wants the solving of these "visual opportunities" to be accomplished through the use of "dynamic design."

This makes me feel good, because in this book, I have constantly used the term dynamic as the end goal for the storyboard artist in every frame of the storyboard.

As a matter of fact I have incorporated many of the design elements, as adapted from my proposed book, *The Conquest of Space* (the progression of spatial design in the history of art as it relates to film and production design). This is what thinking in 3D is all about, and that evolved into this chapter.

The visual field that we encounter is reality, our personal POV. Our virtual reality is in 3D, and as storyboard artists, we want to replicate that reality onto our 2D storyboard frames. This is done through the use of perspective, light and shade, (chiaroscuro, if you will), and sound design techniques, among others.

I heartily recommend Suguru Ishizaki's excellent text, but while it is theoretical (and very valid), this book is practical, practical, practical.

Enjoy!

## Tutorials

1. Study Eisenstein's film form. Look for one- and two-point perspective in shots from his films. Sketch six of each.

2. Render one local street in two-point perspective. Indicate figures in action in the FGD, MGD and BGD.

3. Find a light source and indicate the appropriate shadows.

4. Write two pages of original script. Break it into shots and design a basic storyboard for it.

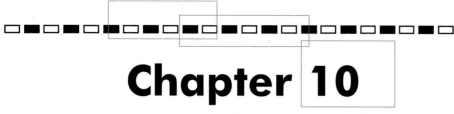

# Chapter 10

## Animatics: The Future of Motion Control

An animatic is an animated storyboard which could be an integral part of the pre-viz process. By their very nature, storyboards are active, vivid pre-viz tools, drawn by the storyboard artist for a given film production. The storyboard is a sequential art, the main goal or purpose of which is to be the visual spine of the screenplay, which then gives the entire preproduction team a visual, sequential breakdown of the main scenes to be filmed.

As if that weren't good enough, about 10 years ago, the animatic appeared on the scene. *Animatics* ("to give life to, to animate"), simply put, brings the storyboards alive with motion and visual effects. You can pace your narrative and your timing and then later add music and dialog.

Animatics are expensive and very time-consuming. My first choice is to create hand-drawn storyboards. If an animatic is requested by the director or producer, the storyboards are turned over to an animatics expert with whom I work closely to ensure the proper selection of scenes.

Why the growing use of animatics for pre-viz of a live action film? With an animatic, it is much easier to demonstrate and fine-tune sequencing, editing and special effects before embarking on the costly filming process.

Animatics use scans, pans, zooms and transitional devices, to give the storyboard an integrated motion control that actually moves the action forward. Now, you get a real preview of the finished shooting script. The storyboard, along with animatics where needed, can be an aid to the pre-viz process of the director, producer, director of cinematography, etc. A musical score could be added to the animatic and, in most cases, actors are used for voice-overs (VO). In the absence of VO, the dialogue could be printed on the appropriate frames.

**ANIMATIC:** A process that gives additional visual movement to a storyboard, re: pans, zooms, montage, etc. – like seeing a preview of a movie. Acts like a visual substitute for SFX in the final movie.

### SEQUENCING

The first step when making an animatic is to select the images directly from the original storyboard. In addition to putting all the frames in order and making sure movement is timed to the script (or soundtrack), the animatic will show transitions between shots. Fades can be used as transitional tools or you might decide, with the film's director, that a "cut to" is more appropriate for the scene. Camera movements are emulated and timed out. For novice filmmakers, making an animatic may indicate that their film is much longer or shorter than anticipated through the scripting and storyboarding stage. If the length of the film or project is an issue, cuts are made or additional material written.

## EDITING

Judicious editing saves time and money when expensive equipment and valuable talent is involved. You can plan ahead or even edit unwanted locales or a scene before actual filming begins, thus saving budget. All the pros say that it's better to edit before rather than afterwards. Why? Often locales or actors aren't available after the shoot. Using animatics further solidifies the preproduction planning and saves time and money while also helping the crew and actors avoid mistakes.

## SPECIAL EFFECTS

An animatic is a "stand-in" for the use of VFX in key storyboard sequences selected by the production team. This SFX could include pyrotechnics, use of miniatures, compositing, matte shots, stop motion or digital doubles (multiplying people digitally), just to name a few.

The amateur might even decide after viewing the animatic that the entire mood or look of the scenes viewed so far aren't working and consequently will make the necessary adjustments to the elements involved.

## A REAL-WORLD ANIMATIC

The following example was done from my storyboards for *The Countess*, Ludovica Villar-Hauser's film version of Gregory Murphy's long-running New York production, both on and off Broadway.

Gregory Murphy aptly summarizes the plot of *The Countess* as being: "Based on a true story, it is set in Venice, London and the Scottish Highlands in the mid-19th century. The art critic John Ruskin invites his protégé, the painter John Everett Millais, to accompany him and his wife Effie on an extended holiday. While away, Millais comes to see that Ruskin, a man he idolizes, emotionally and psychologically torments his wife. The situation is further complicated when Millais realizes he is falling in love with the beautiful young Mrs. Ruskin. The scandal that ensues on their return to London becomes one of the most notorious of the Victorian age."

With those human conflicts in mind, our animatic gives movement and additional dramatic impact to the scenes chosen to visualize the arc of the narrative. With a choice of more than 200 scenes, it was difficult to decide which to choose and so two or three hour-long meetings at my studio were necessary. The first of several meetings with Winnie Tom, the animatics artist, involved going over the storyboards already drawn for Ludovica's film. Winnie also consulted the original film script. (Some changes to that script had been made, but the new storyboards adapted to the changes.)

Once the scenes from the storyboards were decided, Winnie suggested that several scenes could use more close-ups for added dramatic impact and I drew new frames, mostly close-ups of facial reactions and hands. We chose frames or shots that visually told our story. On total view of these scenes from the storyboards of *The Countess*, Winnie's use of pans, transitions and dissolves, as well as her editing, moved the narrative forward, adding to the more dynamic visualization of the script's conflicts, builds, and climaxes. You can view the animatic at www.artofthestory-board.com.

The shots/sequences in Figures 10-1 and 10-2 were finally chosen, and for purposes of this book, are printed directly from the finished animatic. Notice the inclusion of dialogue on some frames.

Frame 1. Establishing shot of Venice

Frame 2. Effie and John Ruskin together and initially happy.

Frame 3. Pan to CU of Effie and John.

Frame 4. Interior night. Ruskin's family dining room with Effie, Ruskin and his parents and servant.

Frame 5. Three shot, Effie in the center feeling uncomfortable. Ruskin is on the right of frame, his father on the left of frame.

Frame 6. Cut to Ruskin's mother being overly critical of Effie's behavior at the ball.

Frame 7. Cut to CU of Ruskin's father doing the same.

Frame 8. An extreme CU of Ruskin looking shocked at Effie's seemingly rude behavior.

Frame 9. Another three-shot of Effie framed by the critical eye of her husband and father-in-law, motivating Effie to leave.

Frame 10. Camera pans Effie as she leaves through door on right of frame, looking upset.

After several viewings, you might decide, as we did, that additional editing could be done.

**Figure 10-1 Animatic frames 1 through 6.**

**Figure 10-2 Animatic frames 7 through 10.**

Looking at the animatic later, we decided to make some changes for the proposed new version. Our new selections are in Figures 10-3 and 10-4. Note that this time, most shots/sequences are taken from the original storyboards and only a couple directly from the finished animatic.

Frame 1. Fade-in night shot, Venice.

Frame 2. Interior night Ruskin's suite. Pan Ruskin's sketches to CU of Ruskin's hand. Continue pan to MS of Ruskin. Note directional arrows.

Frame 3. Interior ballroom. Night. Effie makes her entrance on the grand staircase.

Frame 4. Medium CU of Effie dancing with duke.

Frame 5. Interior CU of Effie gazing into mirror. Ruskin's VO: "scandal"

Frame 6. Medium CU of two-shot of Effie distracting Ruskin.

**Figure 10-3 Storyboard frames 1 through 6.**

**Figure 10-4 Storyboard frames 7 through 12.**

Frame 7. Cut to Scotland. Interior night shot of the rented cottage. CU two-shot, Millais places flowers in Effie's hair.

Frame 8. Two scenes from different angles – 1) CU Millais sketching Effie and 2) Effie in left foreground with Millais sketching her in the BGD right of frame.

Frame 9. Medium CU, Ruskin looks over Millais' shoulder at his sketch of Effie.

Frame 10. OTS, Ruskin critiques Millais' sketch.

Frame 11. CU to exterior night. Camera pans left of frame to right of frame, showing the stormy forest. Cut to a long shot of Millais tent. Cut to a silhouette of Millais working on Ruskin's portrait. Cut to medium shot interior tent where an angry Millais kicks over stove and breaks his paint box on the rocks.

Frame 12. Cut to interior of the cottage. Night. Extreme CU of Effie reacting to the current tensions in her life.

We felt that the newly chosen shot/sequence greatly enhanced the narrative flow of script and could be the basis of another animatic.

Animatics can be a tremendous tool for any script and resultant hand-drawn storyboard. Whenever I see one, I feel that my storyboards just came to life.

## Tutorials

1. Having an animatic produced is expensive, but may be worth the price. If you have a friend who works for a studio that makes animatics, then do a segment of a storyboard that you have drawn.

2. Visit www.animatics.com for more information on animatics, and also check out www.hiroadproductions.com, which has many diverse examples of animatics.

3. Visit www.artofthestoryboard.com to view the animatic for *The Countess.*

# Appendix A
## Additional Resources

Anobile, Richard J., ed. *John Ford's Stagecoach*. Darien House, 1975.

Barber, Barrington. *Advanced Drawing Skills*. Arcturus Foulsham, 2003.

Bare, Richard and Garner, James. *The Film Director: Updated for Today's Filmmaker, the Classic, Practical Reference to Motion Picture and Television Techniques*, Wiley 2001.

Barsacq, Leon. *Caligari's Cabinet and Other Grand Illusions, A History of Film Design*. New American Library, 1978.

Bayer, William. *Great Movies*. Grosset & Dunlap, 1973.

Behlmer, Rudy and Tony Thomas. *Hollywood's Hollywood: The Movies About the Movies*. Citadel Press, 1984.

Belazs, Bela. *Theory of the Film*. Dover Publications, 1970.

Bergala, Alain. *Magnum Cinema*. Phaidon Press, 1995.

Boorstin, Jon. *The Hollywood Eye: What Makes Movies Work*. HarperCollins, 1990.

Box, Harry C. *Set Lighting Technician's Handbook, Third Edition*. Focal Press, 2003.

Bridges, Herb. *The Filming of Gone with the Wind*. Mercer University Press, 1998.

Brownlow, Kevin. *David Lean*. Faber and Faber, 1997.

Burum, Stephen. *American Cinematographer Manual, Ninth Edition*. American Society Of Cinematographers, 2004.

Byrge, Duane, and American Film Institute. *Private Screenings: Insiders Share a Century of Great Movie Moments*. Turner Publications, 1995.

Cameron, James and William Wisher. *Terminator 2: Judgment Day*. Applause Books, 2000.

Capra, Frank. *The Name Above the Title: An Autobiography*. Da Capo Press, 2001.

Castell, David. *Hollywood 1970s*. Gallery Books, 1987.

Chandler, Charlotte. *I, Fellini*. Cooper Square Press, 2001.

Clair, Rene. *Cinema, Yesterday and Today*. Dover Publications, 1972.

Cole, Alison. *Eyewitness Art: Perspective*. Dorling Kindersley, 1992.

Cotto, Mark and Shinji Hata. *From Star Wars to Indiana Jones*. Chronicle Books, 1994.

Dickinson, Thorold. *Discovery of Cinema*. Oxford University Press, 1971.

Dolan, Edward F., Jr. *History of the Movies*. Longmeadow Press, 1986.

Eisenstein, Sergei. *Film Form: Essays in Film Theory*. Harvest Books, 1969.

Farris, Edmond J. *Art Student's Anatomy*. Dover Publications, 1961.

Faulkner, Christopher. *Jean Renoir*. Taschen, 2007.

Field, Syd. *Four Screenplays: Studies in the American Screenplay*. Delta, 1994.

Frayling, Christopher. *Ken Adam: The Art of Production Design*. Faber and Faber, 2006.

Geist, Kenneth. *Pictures Will Talk: The Life and Films of Joseph L Mankiewicz*. Da Capo Press, 1983.

Harris, Robert A. and Michael S. Lasky. *Complete Films of Alfred Hitchcock*. Citadel Press, 2002.

Hart, John. *Lighting for Action*. Amphoto/Watson-Guptill, 1992.

Haver, Ronald. *David O. Selznick's Hollywood*. Random House Value Publishing, 1987.

Hay, Peter. *MGM: When the Lion Roars*. Turner Publishing, 1991.

Henderson, Robert M. *D.W. Griffith: The Years at Biograph*. Farrar, Straus and Giroux, 1970.

Hirsch, Foster. *The Dark Side of the Screen: Film Noir*. Da Capo Press, 2001.

Hirschorn, Clive. *The Hollywood Musical*. Hamlyn, 1991.

Hogarth, Burne. *Dynamic Anatomy, Revised and Expanded Edition*. Watson-Guptill, 2003.

*Hollywood Creative Directory, 59th Edition*. Hollywood Creative Directories, 2007.

Hunter, Fil, Steven Biver, and Paul Fuqua. *Light: Science and Magic: An Introduction to Photographic Lighting*, Third Edition. Focal Press, 2007.

Huss, Roy and Norman Silverstein. *The Film Experience*. Harper & Row, 1968.

Katz, Ephraim. *The Film Encyclopedia, Fifth Edition: The Most Comprehensive Encyclopedia of World Cinema in a Single Volume*. HarperCollins, 2005.

Katz, Steven D. *Film Directing: Shot by Shot*. Michael Wiese Productions/Focal Press, 1991.

Kawin, Bruce F. *How Movies Work*. University of California Press, 1992.

Knight, Arthur. *The Liveliest Art: A Panoramic History of the Movies*. Signet, 1979.

Kolker, Robert. *The Altering Eye: Contemporary International Cinema*. Oxford University Press, 1983.

Konigsberg, Ira. *The Complete Film Dictionary*. Signet, 1998.

Lawton, Richard. *A World of Movies: 70 Years of Film History*. Delacorte Press, 1974.

Leish, Kenneth N. *Cinema*. Newsweek Books, 1974.

Long, Robert Emmet. *The Films of Merchant Ivory*. Harry N. Abrams, 1997.

Maltin, Leonard. *The Art of the Cinematographer*. Dover Publications, 1978.

Marsh, Edward W. and Douglas Kirkland. *James Cameron's Titanic*. HarperCollins, 1997.

Mast, Gerald. *Film/Cinema/Movie: A Theory of Experience*. University of Chicago Press, 1984.

Mordden, Ethan. *The Hollywood Studios*. Alfred A. Knopf, 1988.

*Movies Unlimited Catalog*. Sony Pictures, 2006.

*Multimedia Sourcebook, vol. 3*. WWW, Internet Directory, Hi Tech Media, Inc., 1997.

National Society of Film Critics and Jay Carr. *The A List: The National Society of Film Critics' 100 Essential Films*. Da Capo Press, 2002.

Nelmes, Jill. *An Introduction to Film Studies: Fourth Edition*. Routledge, 2007.

Nowell-Smith, Geoffrey. *The Oxford History of World Cinema*. Oxford University Press, 1999.

Perard, Victor. *Anatomy and Drawing*. New York: Dover Publications, 2004.

Phillips, William H. *Film: An Introduction, Third Edition*. Bedford/St. Martin, 2005.

Pinteau, Pascal. *Special Effects*. Harry Abrams, 2004.

Pirie, David. *Anatomy of the Movies*. Macmillan, 1984.

Place, J. A. *The Non-Western Films of John Ford*. Citadel Press, 1981.

Reisz, Karl and Gavin Millar. *Technique of Film Editing, Second Edition*. Focal Press, 1989.

Renoir, Jean. *My Life and My Films*. Da Capo, 2001.

Robinson, David. *History of World Cinema*. Stein & Day, 1981.

Rogers, Pauline B. *The Art of Visual Effects: Interviews on the Tool of the Trade*. Focal Press, 1999.

Scarfone, Jay and William Stillman. *The Wizardry of Oz, Revised and Expanded Edition*. Applause Books, 2004.

Selznick, David O. (author) Rudy Behlmer (editor). *Memo from David O. Selznick: The Creation of "Gone with the Wind" and Other Motion Picture Classics, as Revealed in the*

*Producer's Private Letters, Telegrams, Memorandums, and Autobiographical Remarks.* Modern Library, 2000.

Sharff, Stefan. *The Elements of Cinema.* Columbia University Press, 1982.

Sherle, Victor and William Turner-Levy. *The Complete Films of Frank Capra.* Carol Publishing Corporation, 1992.

Silver, Alain and James Ursini. *David Lean and His Films.* Silman-James Press, 1991.

Silver, Alain and James Ursini. *The Noir Style.* Gerald Duckworth & Co., 2004.

Sinclair, Andrew. *John Ford: A Biography.* Lorrimer, 1984.

Singer, Michael. *Batman and Robin: Making the Movie.* Rutledge Hill Press, 1997.

Smith, Thomas G. *Industrial Light & Magic: The Art of Special Effects.* Ballentine Books, 1988.

Smith, Thomas Gordon. *Vitruvius on Architecture.* Monacelli, 2003.

Sobchack, Thomas and Vivian Sobchack. *An Introduction to Film, Second Edition.* Longman, 1997.

Sowers, Robert. *Rethinking the Forms of Visual Expression.* University of California Press, 1990.

Sperling, Cass Warner, Cork Millner, and Jack Warner. *Hollywood Be Thy Name: The Warner Brothers Story.* University of Kentucky Press, 1998.

Spoto, Donald. *The Art of Alfred Hitchcock: Fifty Years of His Motion Pictures.* Anchor, 1991.

Spottiswoode, Raymond. *Film and Its Techniques.* University of California Press, 1970.

Stallings, Penny and Howard Mandelbaum. *Flesh and Fantasy.* HarperCollins, 1989.

Talbot, Daniel, ed. *Film: An Anthology, Second Edition.* University of California Press, 1966.

Tashiro, C.S. *Pretty Pictures: Production Design and the History Film.* University of Texas Press, 1998.

Titelman, Carol. *The Art of Star Wars, Episode IV, A New Hope.* Ballantine Books, 1997.

Truffaut, Francois and Helen Scott. *Hitchcock, Truffaut.* Simon and Shuster, 1985.

Valasek, Thomas. *Frameworks: An Introduction to Film Studies.* Thomas Custom Publishing, 2003.

Webb, Michael, ed. *Hollywood: Legend and Reality.* Little Brown and Company, 1986.

Weinberg, Herman G. *The Lubitsch Touch.* Dover Publications, 1977.

Yule, Andrew. *Losing the Light: Terry Gilliam and the Munchausen Saga.* Applause Books, 2000.

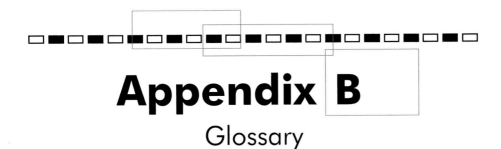

# Appendix B
## Glossary

The following terms are geared to storyboard artists involved in the preproduction/creation of actions depicted in pre-visualization of scenes selected from a script, with visual accent on the actors blocked into a given scene and guided by the director's over-all vision of the film. Please note the sections on Lighting and Camera Angle terms at the end.

Angles: Where to place a camera to best capture a scene. Basic: HI angle, LO angle, normal or straight on angle or a tilted shot. See the angle terms at the end of the glossary.

Animatic: A process that gives additional visual movement to a storyboard, re: pans, zooms, montage, etc.—like seeing a preview of a movie acts as a visual substitute for SFX in the final movie.

Atmospheric perspective: Depth in a scene that does not involve linear perspective but only shades of black, FGD, medium grays, MGD, or vaporous grays in BGD. Can also be referred to as aerial perspective.

Background (BGD): The space occupied by an area furthest back from the foreground.

Blocking: Where the director places the actor within a given scene to convey the action of the script.

Center of interest: Subject of the shot within any of the designated spots that occur when the lines of thirds intersect.

Chiaroscuro: High contrast light and shade as in film noir.

Claymation: Three dimensional stop motion animation using clay figures.

Composite shot: One shot made up of or composed of several different visual elements, i.e., live actors performing in front of CGI visuals, like miniatures, and/or special effects.

Computer graphic imaging (CGI): Imagined and executed scenes created on a computer. For example, in *300*, only the actors were real; all backgrounds and background action were CGI'd and the live action of actors was composited in.

Concept sketch: A "first impression" sketch from one's imagination that visualizes action in scene for the preproduction team. Pencils are great.

Concentric circles: Design factor. Circles or ovals that visually frame the center of interest in a shot.

Continuity: Logical sequence of shots.

Converging lines (orthogonals): All of the straight lines emanating from or going back to the vanishing point that has been positioned on the horizon line or eye level line. Term used in drawings.

Depth of field: The space existing between FGD, MGD, and BGD and selecting what forms should be in sharpest focus in any of these planes.

Divine proportion (golden rectangle): Basically the two-thirds to one-third elongated spacing which dictates a proper well-proportioned rectangle.

Elevator effect: No matter how high we go or how far we move right to left, our eye level, horizon line, and VPs go with us.

Eye level: What we see when we look straight ahead, facing the horizon line.

Film noir: French Term for dark cinema. Popular black and white films mainly from the 40s and 50s. Used chiaroscuro high contrast light and shade.

Focus puller: Director of photography's assistant who, with hand on focal ring of lens, follows the action to keep it in focus at all times.

Forced perspective: Exaggerating the size of FGD elements to cause increased depth in a shot.

Foreground (FGD): Frontal elements that frame the shot.

Framing: Composing the scene within the viewing field of the lens.

Gesture: The basic line of action that occurs when a figure moves.

Head length: Distance from forefinger to wrist.

Horizon line: Line opposite eye level.

Kinetic: Is active, ongoing, dynamic action. It is the opposite of mimetic action.

Linear perspective: Lines that recede to a single vanishing point on the viewer's eye level. Also called perspective lines or orthogonals.

Light plot: Diagram that indicates correct placement of lights for the actors and the scenes in which they appear.

Maquette: Miniature model of a life-sized figure.

Middleground (MGD): the area between the foreground and the background.

Mimetic: Implied action; opposite of kinetic.

Mise-en-scene: Placement of actors within a given scene, tells us visually where the action take place.

Models/miniatures: Rather than going on location, construct a miniature or model in the proper scale, then through CGI, incorporate it into the final composite shot where it appears to be the real full scale original.

Montage: Individual shots or images that conflict with each other (Eisenstein) arranged in a pre-visualized continuity.

Off-center: Actors or action must be away from exact center of a framed shot, and located either to right or left of frame.

One-point perspective: All lines converge to only one point indicated in the horizon line.

Orthogonals: Another term for converging lines.

Overt action: Dynamic action that has a beginning and an end.

Persistence of vision: Retention of an image on the human retina, causing the illusion of motion in films.

Perspective: The art of representing on a two-dimensional plane what the viewer perceives as having three dimensions.

Picasso line: To illustrate the sculptural form of a face it is a line that follows the contours of the face from forehead to neck – resulting also in a "profile" of its own.

Point of view (POV): What the actor sees in the scene, a personal vision.

Postproduction: Editing, sound, addition of VFX, compositing, etc.

Preproduction: Storyboard artist's main activity, working with the production team, involving pre-visualization of elements that will be photographed in continuity.

Pre-visualization (pre-viz): It is the drawings of the storyboard artist that illustrates the visuals that will make up the narrative of the film.

Production: Actual filming of the shooting script: lights, camera, action!

Production sketch: A larger, more complete visualization of a certain scene.

Receding Planes: Areas of space that recede from the FGD, to MGD, to BGD in a scene or shot.

Rule of thirds: Design principle. All framed (within the rectangle) shots are divided into thirds either (or both) vertically or horizontally, resulting in the placement of the center of action at any of the intersections.

Scene: A full visual realization of a narrative action that normally contains a beginning, middle, and end.

Scenario: The storyline of a shooting script; follows the narrative action.

Sequence: A series of shots containing a section of the story-line.

Storyboard: Dear Reader, storyboarding is what this book is all about!

Special effects (SFX): Elements within a scene that are computer generated to give added reality (or unreality) to a scene.

Thumbnail sketch: Small, quick concept sketches, illustrating first ideas.

Two-point perspective: Two separate vanishing points that occur at opposite ends of the horizon line.

Vanishing point: One or two points on the horizon line to which all converging lines will recede.

Visual effects (VFX): Term that has taken the place of Special Effects. Any effect that is not real. Explosions, Superman, Spiderman, or Batman FLIES with no strings! (use of BGD bluescreen or greenscreen). Both are indicated by the storyboard artist.

Voice-over (VO): Actor is off-camera and we only hear the voice.

## LIGHTING

Eye light: Same as fill light, and gives an extra highlight in the actor's eyes, even in the dark.

Diffused light: Softer light on an actor's face, created by putting a soft flame proof material over key lights or the camera lens.

Fill light: An extra light that fills the shadows that result from the key light, also referred to as reflected light or bounce light.

Hair light (also called back light): A light source placed behind the actor to highlight the hair and or figure of an actor this outline of light separates them from the background.

Hi-key lighting: Luminous or brightly lit settings, for comedies, musicals, etc.

Key light: The main light source (usually tungsten/halogen) that lights the actor.

Low key: Lighting darker, with more contrast, stronger light and shadows, for film noir, dramas, suspense, murder mysteries, etc.

Rim light: Side light on an actors face, or placed behind the actor to the left or right of the face.

## CAMERA ANGLES

Close-up (CU): Full face shot of actor(s) or up close shot of objects.

Establishing shot (EST): Shows the placement of the actor(s) for the audience.

Extreme close-up (EXT CU): So close you see only actor's eyes.

Long shot (LS): Shows the actor(s) or objects in the distance (background).

Medium shot (MS): Shows the actor(s) or objects in the MGD.

Over-the-shoulder (OTS): Taken over-the-actors-shoulder; must stay consistent (on same shoulder) for an actor.

Panoramic (pan): The camera moves horizontally to take in a panoramic scene.

Tracking shot: The camera is mounted on wheels and moves smoothly on a track to follow the action. Sometimes a similar "dolly" shot is used, where the camera is pulled or pushed on a cart, like the crab dolly that moves in circular motion.

Zoom shot: The focus goes from wide angle to CU with a zoom lens.

# Index